INHALT

* Unit 6 ist nur Pflichtstoff für den E-Kurs in Nordrhein-Westfalen.

● Diese Aufgabe ist schwieriger.

▸S. 7 Diese Aufgabe kann nach der Erarbeitung der Schülerbuchseite 7 gemacht werden.

Eine Aufgabe, die du in dein Heft schreiben sollst.

Diese Aufgabe löst du mit dem Hörtext auf der Audio-CD.
Die *Listening*-Übungen auf S. 8, 18, 30, 40, 52 und 64 können nur mit der *Workbook*-Audio-CD gelöst werden. Diese *Listenings* sind nicht Bestandteile der Schülerbuch-Audio-CD.

Hier findest du Hilfen, um die englischen Arbeitsanweisungen zu verstehen.

Circle the right answer/word/...	***Kreise*** *die richtige Antwort / das richtige Wort / ...* ***ein.***
Correct the wrong words/...	***Berichtige*** *die falschen Wörter/...*
crossword (across/down)	***Kreuzworträtsel (waagerecht/senkrecht)***
Draw **lines.**	*Zeichne* ***Linien.***
Invent the details / two new questions / ...	***Erfinde die Einzelheiten*** */ zwei neue Fragen / ...*
odd one out	*Etwa:* ***Das unpassende Wort muss raus.***
Tick the right answers/words/...	***Mache ein Häkchen*** *an die richtigen Antworten/ Wörter/...*
Underline ...	***Unterstreiche ...***

Here and there

1 **Niklas didn't listen to his teacher!**
Eight things in his text are wrong – underline them and write the right information.

Britain and Ireland

The biggest country in Britain is Scotland. Scotland and Ireland have borders with England. The Scottish flag is blue and white and the English flag is red and yellow. The capital of Scotland is Aberdeen, and Swansea is the capital of Wales. The most popular sport in Wales is tennis. There's a tunnel from the south of England to France. Ireland is famous for a special beer, and it produces lots of televisions and software.

1 *England*
2 ____________
3 ____________
4 ____________
5 ____________
6 ____________
7 ____________
8 ____________

► S. 7

2 **Read the e-mail from a Scottish boy, Frazer.**
Write an e-mail to Frazer. Tell him about yourself.

Hi! My name is Frazer and I live in Anstruther, in Scotland. I'm 13 and I have a younger brother, Grant. Do you have brothers and sisters? I don't have a pet at home – do you?

I like hip hop music, skateboarding and motorbikes. On Saturday mornings I play football in the school team. What about you?

What subjects do you like at school? Write soon and tell me about yourself!

Bye – Frazer

____
____
____
____
____

► S. 7

Unit 1

London scenes

1 Listen again and tick (✔) <u>all</u> the right answers.

a) In the street. What's the man selling?

T-shirts ☐ bananas ☐ cats ☐ postcards ☐ trainers ☐

b) In a restaurant. What do the people want?

chips ☐ hamburgers ☐ chicken curry ☐ water ☐ juice ☐

▸ S. 8

2 Look at the picture and the words in the box. What can/can't you see in the picture?

bike • boy • bridge • bus • car • cat • dog • girl • ice cream
man • river • road • swimming pool • underground train • woman

I can see *a woman,* ______________________________

____

I can't see ______________________________

____

▸ S. 9

3 a) Circle the odd word out.

city foot town village	listen read teacher write	child cinema restaurant shop

b) Make *odd word out* games for your partner.

▸ S. 9

4 Who's Asha?
Finish the text with the words in the box.

are staying • lives • misses • 're looking • 's starting • writes

Asha is from Singapore, but now she ________ in London. Asha and her family ________ ________ with her aunt at the moment, but they ________ for their own place. Asha is nervous because she ________ her new school soon. She often ________ to her friend Per Li in Singapore – she ________ Per Li very much.

▸ S. 10

5 Find eleven words and write them in the right lists.

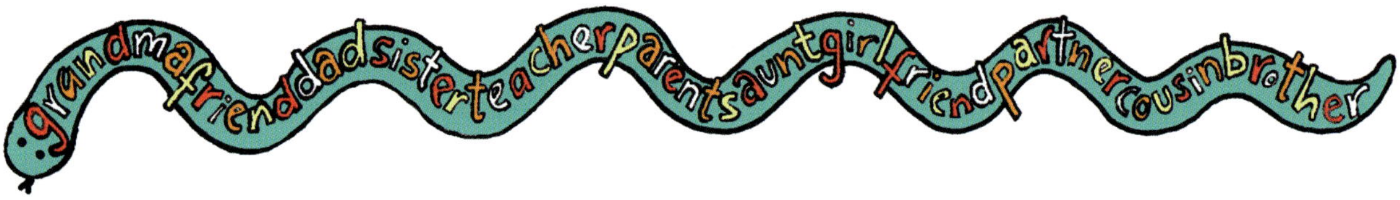

Family	Not family
________	________
________	________
________	________

▸ S. 10

6 Songs. Finish these sentences.

My favourite *(band/singer)* ________ at the moment is ________ ________. My favourite song is ________.

I hate *(band/singer)* ________.

▸ S. 11

7 London Quiz. Answer the questions with the words in the box.

the Olympics • Piccadilly Circus • the Queen • the river in London

1 Who lives in Buckingham Palace? ________

2 What's happening in 2012? ________

3 What's the Thames? ________

4 What's the name of a famous place in London? ________

▸ S. 11

Don't give up!

8 **Make sentences about Asha. Draw lines.**

1 Monday is Asha's	Singapore, in Asia.
2 Asha comes from	the music club.
3 Asha likes Lara,	first day at school.
4 It isn't easy to find	school radio programme.
5 Asha joins	but Lara has other friends.
6 They start a	new friends.

▸ S. 13

9 **Read *scene 2: The noticeboard.* Then look at sentences 1–5.**
Find the wrong word in every sentence. Underline it and give the right word.

1 Asha is feeling happy. ______________

2 She's talking to Mr Nixon, the new teacher. ______________

3 Mr Nixon says Asha shouldn't join a club. ______________

4 Asha doesn't like any groups. ______________

5 They look at the school newspaper and see some good clubs. ______________

▸ S. 13

10 **You're at a new school. Write to your friend in your old town.**
Use the words in the box or invent the details.

aunt / every Friday / last Monday / lunchtime /
modern / music / nervous / nice / some CDs

Dear ______________ *(give the name of your friend)*,

I'm staying with my ______________ at the moment.

______________ was my first day at my new school and I felt ______________.

The school is very ______________, and the people in my class are ______________.

We're starting a ______________ club. It meets ______________

at ______________. I'm sending you ______________. Write soon!

______________ *(give your name)*

▸ S. 13

11 Find the missing words and then do the crossword.

1

2

3

4

5

1 There's an important test at school today. I'm feeling ...

2 Do you go to school by bus? – No, I go by ... train.

3 The weather is terrible. It's very ...

4 What ... are you from? – I'm from Singapore.

5 Don't work alone. Work in a ...

			1					O	U				
2								O	U				
					3			O	U				
						4		O	U				
					5			O	U				

▸ S. 14

12 Asha is writing to her cousin. Put in *some* or *any*.

There are ________ Asian pupils at my new school, but there aren't ________ people from Singapore. I haven't joined ________ clubs yet, but the school has ________ interesting activities. We've all bought ________ warm clothes because it's very cold here. Now we don't have ________ money! I'm sending you ________ photos of my new friends, but I don't have ________ photos of the school yet.

▸ S. 14

13 What's Mr Nixon saying to Asha? Finish the sentences with the words from the box.

Hello, Asha. Are you feeling ____________ here in your new school?

I know it isn't ________ to find new friends, but don't ________ up.

You should ________ a club. Let's look at the ________________.

Do you like ____________?

- easy
- give
- join
- lonely
- music
- noticeboard

▸ S. 14

14 **Write the words in the right networks. Then find more words for the networks.**

exciting | art | fruit | funny
great | history | juice | ~~maths~~ | sandwiches

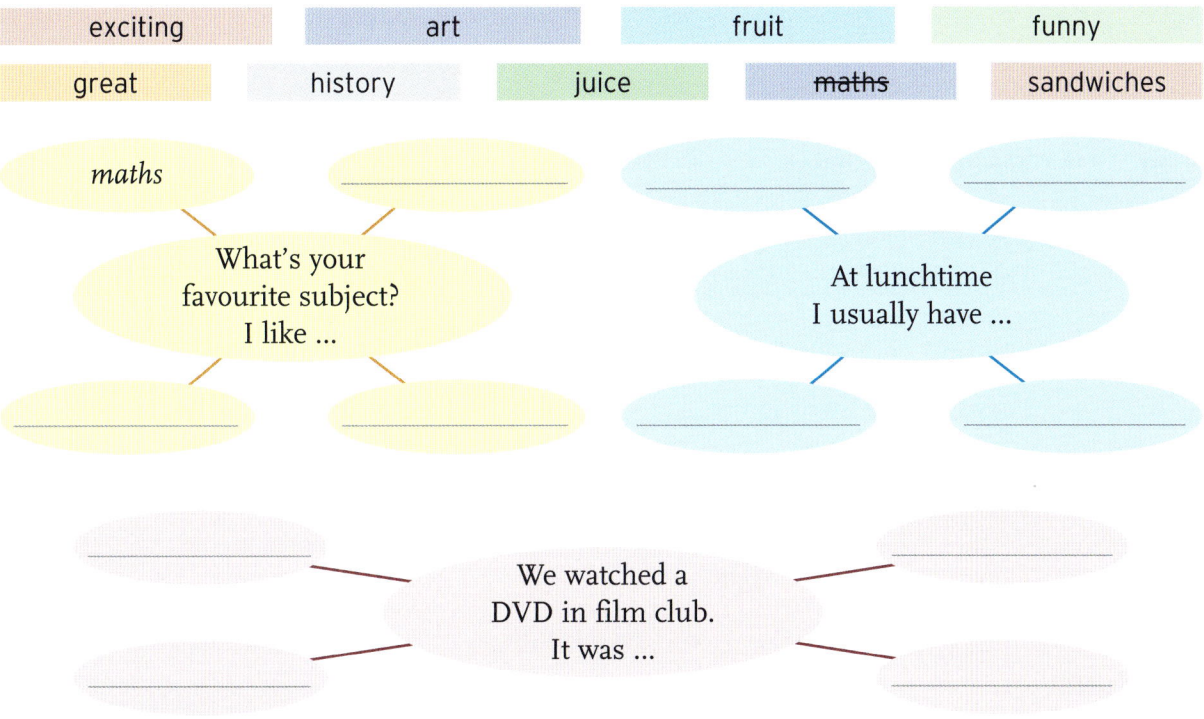

What's your favourite subject? I like ...
- *maths*
- ____
- ____
- ____

At lunchtime I usually have ...
- ____
- ____
- ____
- ____

We watched a DVD in film club. It was ...
- ____
- ____
- ____
- ____

▸ S. 15

15 **Small words. Circle the right word.**

Hi! Thanks *for/of* your e-mail.
I live *in/at* London *for/with* my parents and sister.
Here's a photo *of/to* our house.
Our school is next *at/to* a park, and *in/at* lunchtime we play football there.

▸ S. 15

16 **a) What clubs are there in your school?**

There's a / There isn't a | music/computer/... | club.
There aren't any clubs.

____

____

● **b) What clubs would you like to go to? Why?**

I'd like to go to ____ because ____

____

▸ S. 15

17 LISTENING

Listen to the four dialogues and tick (✓) the right answers.

1 Where do the people want to go?

- **a)** ☐ The Millennium Bridge
- **b)** ☐ Westminster Station
- **c)** ☐ Big Ben
- **d)** ☐ The London Eye

2 How can the people get to Big Ben?

- **a)** ☐ They turn left then right.
- **b)** ☐ They turn left then left.
- **c)** ☐ They turn right then left.
- **d)** ☐ They turn right then right.

3 How much are tickets for children?

- **a)** ☐ £11
- **b)** ☐ £11.50
- **c)** ☐ £7
- **d)** ☐ £7.50

4 How many tickets does the man buy?

- **a)** ☐ 2 tickets
- **b)** ☐ 3 tickets
- **c)** ☐ 4 tickets
- **d)** ☐ 5 tickets

▸S. 16

18 SPEAKING

a) Make the dialogue. Finish the sentences. Use the words in the box.

are • can (2x) • get • have to • queue • repeat

A Excuse me, please. Where ________ I ________ tickets for Buckingham Palace?

B You ______________________ up here.

A And how much ________ the tickets, please?

B £14 for adults and £8 for children under 17.

A Sorry. ________ you ________ that, please?

B Adults £14 and children under 17 £8.

A Thanks.

b) Invent a dialogue with a partner. Write it in your exercise book. Then act the dialogue.

▸S. 17

19 INTERPRETING

You're in London. A police officer tells you how to get to the British Museum. Tell your sister in German.

Take the tube to Euston Square. Go along Gower Street. Turn left at Great Russell Street. The museum is on the left.

Sie sagt, wir sollen mit der ______________________________________.

Wir sollen ______________________________. Wir sollen ______________________

______________________. ______________________________________.

▸S. 17

20 READING

a) Read the text about a famous book.

TOM'S MIDNIGHT GARDEN

by Philippa Pearce

Tom's Midnight Garden is an exciting story about a 12-year-old boy, Tom. It's the summer holidays and he's staying at his aunt's flat. It's very boring.

One night Tom can't sleep. Suddenly the clock *(= Uhr)* strikes *(= schlägt)* 13! 13 o'clock?! Tom goes into the garden ... and into the past! In the garden, the year is 1880!

In the garden, Tom meets Hatty, an orphan – she has no mother or father. She isn't very happy. Tom goes to the garden every night to meet his new friend ...

b) Which sentences are right (✔)? Which sentences are wrong (✘)?

1 The book is about an old man. ☐

2 The book is very boring. ☐

3 Tom is staying with his aunt. ☐

4 At night Tom goes into the past. ☐

5 Tom meets Hatty in the flat. ☐

6 Hatty lives with her parents. ☐

► S. 19

21 WRITING

Write notes about *Tom's Midnight Garden*.

Title: ______

Writer: ______

Who: ______

Story: Tom is staying ______.

One night he goes ______ and ______, and meets ______.

What the book is like: ______.

► S. 19

● 22 Look at this picture from a film. Write notes. Invent some details.

Title: ______

Who: ______

Story: ______

______

______

What the film is like: ______

Watch Tara Patel's
Monsters in 2099
– you'll love it.

► S. 19

CHECKPOINT

Die Gegenwart
Trage hier den Checkpoint aus dem Schülerbuch (Seite 21) ein und schreibe deine eigenen Beispiele und Beispielsätze auf.

Mit der einfachen Gegenwart *(simple present)* sagst du, ______________________________

____

Beispiel: I ____________ football every Monday.

Mein Beispielsatz:

____

Mit der *ing*-Form der Gegenwart *(present progressive)* sagst du, ______________________

____

Beispiel: I __________________ a book now.

Mein Beispielsatz:

____

▸ S. 21

23 Simple present.
Finish the sentences about Mr and Mrs Coe.
Use the words in the box.

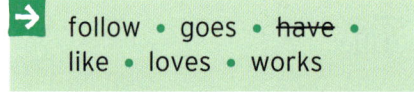

follow • goes • ~~have~~ • like • loves • works

Mr and Mrs Coe *have* six cats. Mrs Coe ___________ all animals, but Mr Coe doesn't ___________ dogs. Mrs Coe ___________ in a hospital. Every day she _________ to work at 8 a.m. – and the cats ___________ her to the hospital door!

▸ S. 21

24 Simple present.
Circle the right form of the verb.

ALI Where does your cousin Becky *live/lives*?

JOE She *live/lives* in Singapore, and she *go/goes* to an international school there. Her parents *work/works* for a bank in Singapore. They *don't/doesn't* come back to England often.

ALI Does Becky *like/likes* Singapore?

JOE Yes, but she *don't/doesn't* like the weather in November and December – it rains a lot.

▸ S. 21

25 Present progressive.
What are their plans? Put in *'m, 're, is, are* and the verb *(-ing)*.

AMY What *are* you *doing (do)* this evening?

JESS I ______________________ *(stay)* at home.

ELLIE We ______________________ *(go)* to the cinema.

Do you want to come? Joe ______________________ *(come)* too.

JESS I can't. I ______________________ *(look)* after my brother –

my parents ______________________ *(go)* to a party.

▸ S. 21

26 What are these people doing at this moment?

He ______________________ ______________________ ______________________

______________________ ______________________ ______________________

▸ S. 21

27 a) Simple present or present progressive? Circle the right form of the verb.

Hannah loves sport. She*'s going / goes* to the badminton club every week.

Today she*'s playing / plays* in a match. The teams *play / are playing* very well this afternoon.

But Hannah and her partner *are usually winning / usually win* – and they*'re winning / win* now!

● **b) Write the right form of the verb.**

Kieran likes music. At the moment he ______________________ *(learn)* the saxophone.

He ______________________ *(play)* the guitar too. Next Saturday he's singing with a band.

I ______________________ *(go)* to their concert next week. I ______________________

(often go) to concerts. I ______________________ *(love)* music. I ______________________ *(sing)*,

but I ______________________ *(not play)* the guitar.

▸ S. 21

TEST YOURSELF

1 Put in *some* or *any*.

There are ________ good clubs at school. I don't like ________ sports, but I've joined the music club. We don't have ________ money, but we have ________ good CDs. We've made ________ posters. There are 20 students in the club, but there aren't ________ teachers.

2 Asking for information. Make questions. Draw lines.

1 Excuse me, can you	I get tickets for the London Eye?
2 How do we get	help me, please?
3 Where can	the tickets, please?
4 Can you repeat	to Big Ben?
5 How much are	that, please?

3 Write the verbs in the present progressive.

Hi Gemma,

We're staying (stay) with my cousins in Wales.

I ____________ (have) lots of fun here.

We ____________ (sit) on the beach at the moment and my cousin ____________ (play) his guitar.

My parents ____________ (buy) some ice cream.

________ you ____________ (go) on holiday this summer?

Joanne

4 Simple present. Circle the right words.

My dad is a teacher. He *goes/go* to school by car.
I *doesn't/don't* go to my dad's school:
I *go/goes* to a school nearer our house.
My sisters *doesn't/don't* go to school –
they *go/goes* to work.
What school *does/do* you go to?

▸ Auf der Seite 69 findest du die Lösungen.

Unit 2

Scottish stories

1 Listen again and circle the right answers.

a) Lauren and Callum

1 The film was *2 1/2 hours* / *3 1/2 hours* long with all the adverts.

2 The first part was *boring/romantic*.

3 Callum thought the music was *great/terrible*.

b) Mum and Fiona

1 Fiona's mum *likes* / *doesn't like* romantic films.

2 Fiona thought the film was *silly/great*.

3 The funny parts of the film were about *England/Scotland*.

▸S. 22

2 a) Match the questions with the answers. Two answers are right for one question. Write the letters.

1 What films do you like? *d* ____

2 Did you watch a film this month? ____ ____

3 Where did you watch it? ____ ____

4 Was it good? ____ ____

5 Who did you watch it with? ____ ____

a) I watched it on DVD.

b) Yes, I watched a film about history.

c) I watched it with my sister.

d) I love exciting films.

e) At the cinema.

f) My dad and I watched it together.

g) No, it wasn't. It was long and boring.

h) I like romantic films.

i) Yes, it was. It was very funny.

j) No, I didn't watch any films.

b) AND YOU? Write the questions in exercise 2a in your exercise book. Answer them. Invent two new questions and answer them too.

▸S. 23

3 Answer these questions about Fiona.

1 How old is Fiona? — She's ______________.

2 What's her favourite place? — Her favourite place is ______________.

3 When did she go there with Emma? — She ______________.

4 What sport does Fiona play? — She ______________.

5 Where does she practise? — ______________

6 What club did she join last year? — ______________

▸ S. 24

4 Read these phrases. Which three words are right (✔)?

1 an old ...

☐ month ☐ film ☐ shopping ☐ castle ☐ city

2 a Scottish ...

☐ actor ☐ city ☐ free time ☐ age ☐ football team

3 a silly ...

☐ capital ☐ film ☐ file ☐ name ☐ article

4 a famous ...

☐ weekend ☐ street ☐ actor ☐ interest ☐ castle

5 the film is ...

☐ sad ☐ nervous ☐ romantic ☐ underground ☐ silly

6 I play football in ...

☐ a team ☐ the park ☐ the cupboard ☐ my free time ☐ Big Ben

▸ S. 24

5 Star file: Katie Leung. Draw lines. Then write the sentences in your exercise book.

1 Katie Leung is an →	Motherwell in Scotland.
2 She was born	shopping with friends.
3 She's from	actor.
4 Katie is interested	in 1987.
5 She loves to go	in music and art.
6 She has	married.
7 She isn't	the Harry Potter films.
8 Her best films are	two brothers and one sister.

▸ S. 25

Best friends?

6 Think about the story again. Put the pictures in the right order. Write the numbers 2–6.

▸ S. 27

7 Write sentences with *because*.

Fiona was jealous She walked home alone She went to her room Lauren wanted to take Fiona to the film Fiona was embarrassed	because	she didn't want to talk to Lauren. Fiona was a fan of Ewan McGregor. she wanted to invite Callum to the cinema. Lauren won the competition. her mum wasn't at home.

1 Fiona was jealous ______________________________.

2 She walked home alone ______________________________.

3 She went to her room ______________________________.

4 ______________________________

5 ______________________________

▸ S. 27

8 On Saturday Fiona and Callum went to the cinema.
What did Fiona say to her friends on Sunday?

On Saturday I went ____________________ with ____________________.

We watched ______________________________.

It was ______________________________.

Callum is ______________________________.

▸ S. 27

9 Pick the right words. Circle them.

"I live in Stirling, an old Scottish *chat/city*. It has a big *castle/capital*, and there are some great *shops/ships* in the town centre. In my free *time/file* I play basketball. We *problem/practise* every Friday. Our team sometimes wins *congratulations/competitions*!"

► S. 28

10 How did Maryam feel? Write the right words.

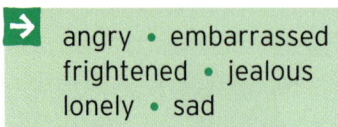

→ angry • embarrassed • frightened • jealous • lonely • sad

1

When she saw a big spider, she felt ______________.

2 When a silly boy hurt Maryam's cat, she was very ______________.

3 When Sima won the competition, Maryam was very ______________.

4 The teacher read Maryam's poem to the class. Maryam felt very ______________.

5 Her parents were out yesterday. Maryam was ______________.

6

Maryam's hamster died. She felt ______________.

► S. 28

11 a) Finish the dialogue. Put in *much* or *many*.

LEE Do you have ______________ friends in Germany?

JACK I have two German friends, but I don't have ______________ time to write letters.

LEE Do you know ______________ German history?

JACK Yes – there are so ______________ interesting stories!

LEE I'd like to go to Germany, but I don't have ______________ money at the moment.

● **b) Write six sentences with *much* and *many* in your exercise book.**

Do you ...? / I don't / We/...	have/ watch/ play/...	much many	free time / nice cafes / CDs / homework / sport / good shops / films / ...	at the moment. / in our/your town. / ...

► S. 28

12 a) Read the file about Wales.

Info file: Wales

Wales is part of Great Britain, but it isn't part of England. Wales is a different country with its own history.

Some Welsh (= *walisisch)* people speak two languages. Everybody in Wales speaks English, of course. But some people speak Welsh too – at home, at work and in school.

Tourists often ask: "What money does Wales use?" Is it the euro? No. Like England and Scotland, Wales uses the pound.

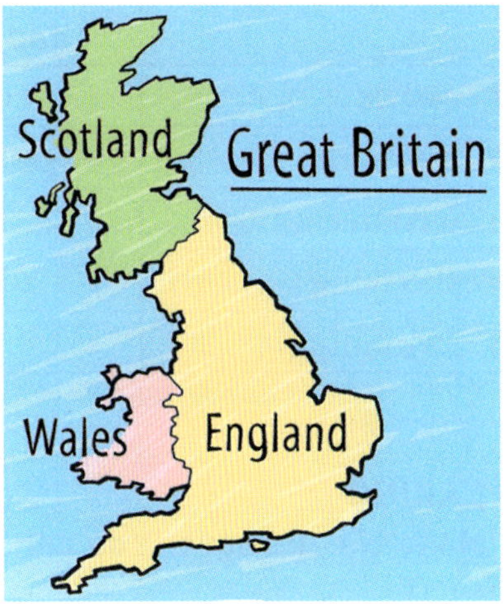

Many sports and interests are popular in Wales. Rugby and fishing are the most popular sports. Music is very popular too.

b) Make notes about the most important information.

Wales: *part of* ______________________

Wales: *not part of* ______________________

Languages: ______________________

Money: ______________________

Sports: ______________________

Other interests: ______________________

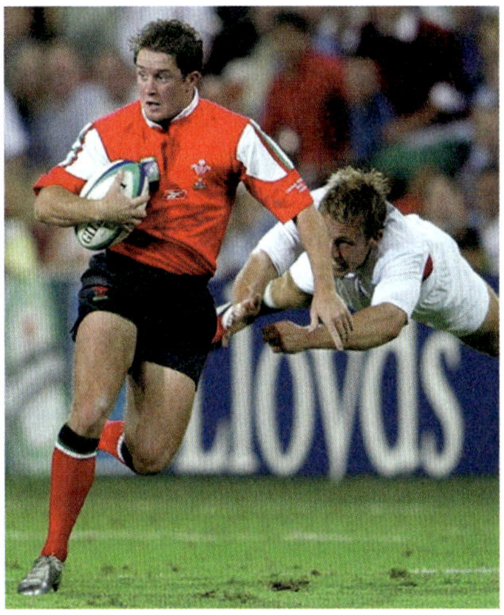

▸S. 29

● 13 Read the notes. Make an info file about Luxembourg in your exercise book.

- *Luxembourg:*
  not part of France; different country
- *Languages:*
  Luxembourgish, French, German
- *Money:*
  euro
- *Popular sports:*
  football, tennis, volleyball

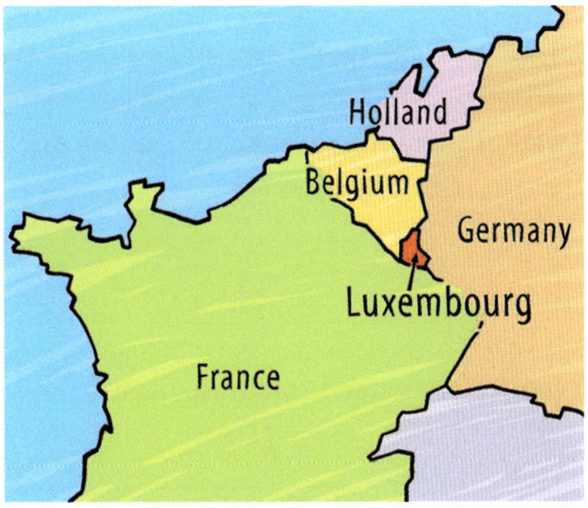

▸S. 29

14 LISTENING

Amy and her dad are going to Edinburgh for the weekend.
Listen to the CD: Who likes what (✓)?

	dad	Amy
1 castles		
2 museums		
3 old streets		
4 shopping		
5 swimming		

▸ S. 30

15 SPEAKING

a) Make the dialogue. You can use the ideas in the box.

A Would you like to ______________ on ______________?

B I'm afraid I'm visiting my grandma then.

A What about ______________ ______________?

B That's fine. Why don't we meet at my house at ____ o'clock?

A Great!

go shopping / go swimming / play football / watch a DVD / ...

Saturday / Sunday / morning / afternoon / evening / ...

b) Invent a dialogue with a partner. Write it in your exercise book. Then act the dialogue.

▸ S. 31

16 INTERPRETING

Ewan, a Scottish friend, is staying with you.
Tell your brother what Ewan is saying to him.

EWAN I love playing football.

YOU Er sagt, er ______________.

EWAN Do you like computer games?

YOU Er fragt, ob du ______________.

EWAN I like funny films, but I'm not keen on films about history.

YOU Er meint, ______________

______________.

EWAN I can't stand romantic films!

YOU Er sagt, ______________.

▸ S. 31

17 READING

a) Read the letter.

Dear Hi Magazine,
I want to tell you about my grandad. He loves swimming. Last year I went on holiday with my grandad and my grandma.
On the first day grandad and I went swimming in the sea. It was fun. Suddenly there was a big wave – and grandad's false teeth fell into the water! We looked for them on the beach – we looked and looked – but didn't find them. Poor grandad! He was very embarrassed because he had no teeth all holiday. But grandma and I laughed and laughed – it was so funny!
Sam Tyler (14), Swindon

b) Answer the questions.

1 Who? ____________________

2 When? ____________________

3 Where? ____________________

4 What? ____________________

c) WRITING
Read the notes. Write a letter in your exercise book. Sam's letter can help you.

Dear Hi Magazine,
I want to tell you about my ...
Last ... I went fishing with ... on the ...
It was fun! Suddenly ...

Who?	My dad
When?	Last weekend
Where?	On the river Exe
What?	We went fishing. Dad fell into the water.

▸S. 32

18 What do the text messages say?

Can U read 'text'?!

2 = to	L8 (L+8) = late	B = be	U = you
4 = for	W8 (W+8) = wait	C = see	

1 DO U WANT 2 DANCE?
____

2 C U 2MORROW
____

3 W8 4 ME
____

4 I LOVE U
____

5 DON'T B L8
____

6 COME 4 TEA
____

▸S. 32

CHECKPOINT

Simple past **(1)**
Trage hier die Checkpoints aus dem Schülerbuch (Seite 34/35) ein und schreibe deine eigenen Beispiele und Beispielsätze auf.

Mit dem *simple past* sagst du, ____________________

Damit kannst du ____________________

Regelmässige Verben enden auf ______. Beispiele: ____________________

Unregelmässige Verben ____________________

Beispiele: ____________________

Simple past **(2):** ***did/didn't***

Mit ______ fragst du, was geschehen ist. Mit ______ sagst du, was nicht geschehen ist.

Meine Beispielsätze: ____________________

____

▸ S. 34–35

19 Read the text. Write the missing words.

bought • did • drank • made • read • thought • was

Robert Louis Stevenson ______ a famous Scottish writer. I ______ his book, *Doctor Jekyll and Mr Hyde*, and I ______ it on holiday. I ______ it was exciting! In the story, Dr Jekyll was very interested in science. He ______ a special drink. When he ______ it, he became Mr Hyde – and he ______ terrible things!

▸ S. 35

20 Put the words in the right order. Write the dialogue.

MUSTAFA did / What / yesterday / you / do ____________________

STEVE the cinema / went / I / with my dad / to ____________________

MUSTAFA you / did / What / the film / think of ____________________

STEVE didn't / film / the / I / like ____________________

It / exciting / very / wasn't ____________________

▸ S. 35

21 **Crossword.**
Write the verbs in the simple past.

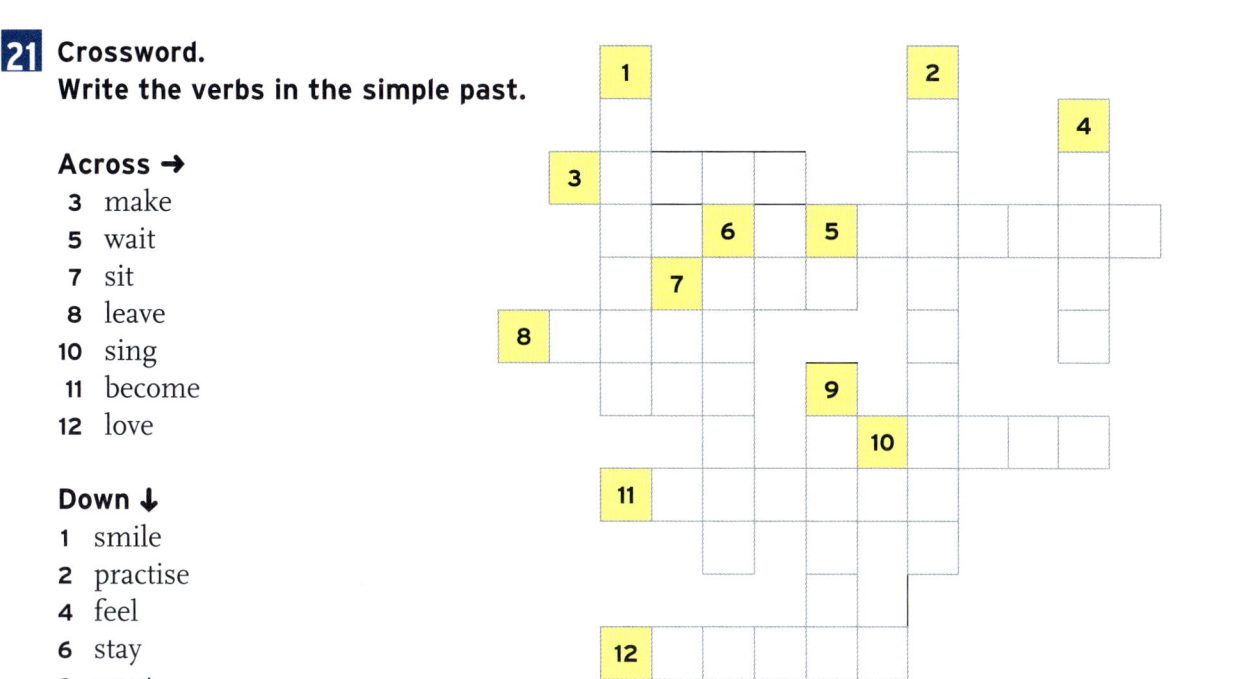

Across →
3 make
5 wait
7 sit
8 leave
10 sing
11 become
12 love

Down ↓
1 smile
2 practise
4 feel
6 stay
9 want

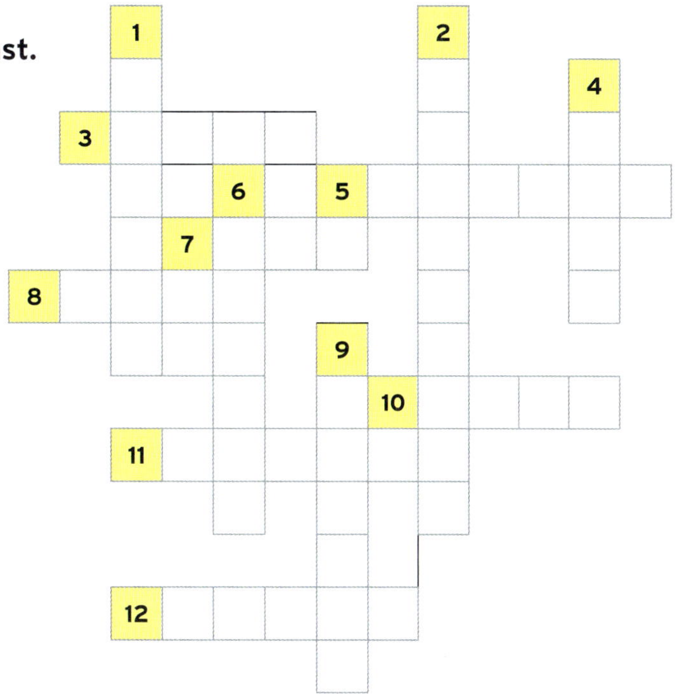

▸ S. 35

22 **a) A holiday on Skye. Write the verbs in the simple past.**

ELLA What ___________ you ___________ *(do)* in the holidays?

AMY We ______________ *(visit)* my aunt and uncle on Skye.

ELLA How long ___________ you ___________ *(stay)* there?

AMY We ______________ *(stay)* a week. It was cold, but it

______________ *(not rain)*.

ELLA ___________ you ___________ *(go)* to the beach?

AMY Yes. We ______________ *(swim)* every day. It ___________ *(be)* a great holiday! But we

______________ *(not see)* the Highland Games – we _________ *(have)* to go home that day.

b) AND YOU? Write three sentences about what you did in the holidays.
You can use the words in the boxes or invent your own sentences.

... bought | ... listened | ... played | ... stayed | ... went

... beach | ... CDs | ... cinema | ... clothes | ... football | ... friends

... home | ... ice cream | ... music | ... radio | ... shopping

____.

____.

____.

▸ S. 35

TEST YOURSELF

1 *Much* or *many*? Put in the right word.

ANNIE Glasgow is great! It has so ______ good shops.
I love shopping, but I don't have ______ free time.

LEE How ______ people live in Glasgow?

ANNIE About 590,000. It's a big city.

LEE I like shopping too, but I have too ______ homework – and I don't have ______ money!

2 Put the sentences in the right order. Write the numbers 1–5.

[ ] **RYAN** That's fine. Why don't we meet at my house at 7 o'clock?
[ ] **LUKE** Would you like to watch a film on Friday?
[ ] **LUKE** Great!
[ ] **LUKE** What about Saturday?
[ ] **RYAN** I'm afraid I'm going to a party on Friday.

3 Read Harry's e-mail. Which sentences are right (✔)? Which sentences are wrong (✘)?

At the weekend I sometimes go to the cinema. I love funny films. I'm not keen on sad films, but my mum likes them. And I can't stand romantic films – they're silly. I like exciting action films. I often watch DVDs. DVDs are great – you can watch films in different languages! What films do you like?
Harry

1 Harry can't stand funny films. [ ]
2 He doesn't like sad films. [ ]
3 He hates romantic films. [ ]
4 He isn't keen on action films. [ ]
5 He likes DVDs. [ ]

4 Last Saturday. Write the verbs. Use the simple past.

HOLLY Where ______ you ______ *(go)* last Saturday?

ROBIN I ______ *(go)* to the sports centre. My parents ______ *(be)* with me, but my brother ______ *(not come)*.

HOLLY What ______ you ______ *(do)*?

ROBIN We ______ *(play)* badminton and I ______ *(buy)* a new T-shirt. Then we ______ *(watch)* a volleyball match – but my team ______ *(not win)*.

▸ Auf den Seiten 69–70 findest du die Lösungen.

PORTFOLIO

Hier kannst du darüber nachdenken, was du in den Units 1 und 2 schon alles gelernt hast.

Das kann ich!

Male die Kästchen aus. Leer bedeutet „das muss ich noch üben" ☐, halb ausgemalt bedeutet „das kann ich mit Hilfe" ◧ und vollständig ausgemalt bedeutet „das kann ich bereits gut" ■.

Unit 1

Ich kann zwei Sätze mit *some* und zwei Sätze mit *any* bilden. ☐
(Tipp: Schau dir die Übung 12 auf Seite 6 an.)

Ich kann fragen, wo es Eintrittskarten gibt und wie viel sie kosten. ☐
(Tipp: Schau dir die Übung 18 auf Seite 8 an.)

Ich kann englische Wegbeschreibungen auf Deutsch wiedergeben. ☐
(Tipp: Schau dir die Übung 19 auf Seite 8 an.)

Ich kann Notizen zu einem Buch oder einer Geschichte machen, z. B. *title/writer/story/...* ☐
(Tipp: Schau dir die Übungen 21–22 auf Seite 9 an.)

Ich kann in vier Sätzen sagen, was jemand immer wieder oder regelmäßig tut, z. B. *She lives in Singapore.* ☐
(Tipp: Schau dir die Übung 24 auf Seite 10 an.)

Ich kann in vier Sätzen sagen, was ich gerade tue oder plane, z. B. *I'm staying at home this evening.* ☐
(Tipp: Schau dir die Übung 25 auf Seite 11 an.)

Der Titel meiner Arbeit für das Portfolio lautet:

____

Unit 2

Ich kann in fünf Sätzen etwas über meinen Lieblings-Film- oder Popstar sagen. ☐
(Tipp: Schau dir die Übung 5 auf Seite 14 an.)

Ich kann zwei Sätze mit *much* und zwei Sätze mit *many* bilden. ☐
(Tipp: Schau dir die Übung 11 auf Seite 16 an.)

Ich kann das Wichtigste in einem Text erkennen und davon Notizen machen. ☐
(Tipp: Schau dir die Übung 12 auf Seite 17 an.)

Ich kann mich verabreden und dabei Ort und Zeitpunkt besprechen. ☐
(Tipp: Schau dir die Übung 15 auf Seite 18 an.)

Ich kann in fünf Sätzen etwas über meine letzten Ferien erzählen. ☐
(Tipp: Schau dir die Übung 22 auf Seite 21 an.)

Der Titel meiner Arbeit für das Portfolio lautet:

____

Tipp: Du kannst auch deine Lehrerin / deinen Lehrer fragen, welche Fortschritte du im Englischunterricht gemacht hast.

Das kann ich auch noch!

Ich kenne fünf Wörter, die mit „Stadt" zu tun haben, z. B. *street, bus.*
(Tipp: Schau dir Seite 9 im Schülerbuch an.)

Ich kenne vier Adjektive, die einen Film beschreiben, z. B. *funny.*
(Tipp: Schau dir Seite 22 im Schülerbuch an.)

Vokabeln lernen

Welche der Methoden helfen dir am besten beim Lernen neuer Vokabeln? Kreuze an.
Nutze demnächst doch mal eine Methode, die du noch nie angewendet hast!

	Hilft mir	Hilft mir nicht	Habe ich noch nie probiert
Ich spreche mir die Wörter laut vor.			
Ich schreibe die Wörter auf.			
Ich male ein Bild zu den Wörtern.			
Ich verwende die neuen Wörter in einem Satz.			
Ich schreibe Wörter nach Themen, nach Wortfamilien, nach Listen oder in Wortnetzen *(networks)* auf.			
Ich bitte jemanden, mich abzufragen.			
Ich teste mich selbst, indem ich mit Vokabellisten arbeite und dabei abwechselnd die deutsche oder die englische Seite verdecke.			
Ich schreibe schwierige Wörter auf Karten und hänge sie in mein Zimmer, damit ich sie immer wieder lesen kann.			
Ich spreche schwierige Wörter auf einen MP3-Player oder ein Handy und teste mich so selbst.			

Lerntipp

Vokabeln falten – Auch diese Methode hilft dir beim Einprägen neuer Wörter.

1 Nimm ein DIN-A4-Blatt quer und schreibe ganz links die englischen Wörter (oder Sätze) untereinander, die du lernen möchtest.

2 Die deutschen Bedeutungen schreibst du daneben.

3 Jetzt faltest du die englischen Wörter nach hinten, sodass nur noch die deutschen Vokabeln zu sehen sind.

4 Schreibe nun wieder die englischen Bedeutungen neben diese Wörter.

5 Verfahre abwechselnd so weiter bis das Blatt voll ist.

Unit 3

Wild Wales

1 Listen again and read the sentences. Correct the wrong word in every sentence.

1 “We’re near the river – the Afon Glaslyn – it’s over there on the ~~left~~.” ____________

2 “This is the ~~tourist office~~ on the left, near the River Garden restaurant.” ____________

3 “Now we’re at the bridge. It’s very old. Let’s wait for a minute – a ~~car~~ is coming.” ____________

4 “That’s a ~~fine~~ hotel on the left – the Tanronnen Hotel ... It’s very old.” ____________

5 “Now look over there. On the left, in that ~~shop~~ you can see Gelert’s Grave.” ____________

▸S. 36

2 Write the words from the box in the right lists. Find three more words for every list.

castle • chicken • children • friends • ice cream
sports centre • tourist office • tourists • vegetables

place	people	food

▸S. 36

3 Finish the text with the words in the box.

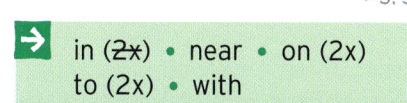

in (~~2x~~) • near • on (2x)
to (2x) • with

Here we are *in* Beddgelert. We’re standing ________ the river – the Afon Glaslyn. Next ________ the river you can see the school. And this is the post office ________ the left. You can get nice cakes ________ the cafe over there. I often go ________ the cafe – I go there on Saturdays ________ my friends. Oh look! There’s a cat ________ the bridge!

▸S. 37

4 **Read Aled's blog again and answer the questions.**

1 Where does Aled live?

He lives ______________________.

2 What's it like there in winter?

____

3 What business do his parents have?

____

4 Why does Aled have to speak English at home?

____

5 Why doesn't Aled have a TV?

____

► S. 38

5 **a) Finish the words and write them in the right box.**

~~n?c?~~ | ?nt?r?st?ng | b?r?ng | sp?c??l | t?rr?bl? | b?d | ?xc?t?ng | ? w?st? ?f t?m? | gr??t

☺ It's ...	☹ It's ...
nice, ______________________	______________________
______________________	______________________

b) Write about two hobbies you like and one hobby you don't like. Say why. Exercise 5a can help you.

I like ______________________. I think it's ______________________.

____

____

● **c) Write two sentences about school subjects, films or food you like and two sentences about things you don't like. Say why.**

______________________.

______________________.

______________________.

______________________.

► S. 39

Parents are a pain!

6 Read the story again. Are the sentences right (✔) or wrong (✘)?

1 Aled's parents said Aled couldn't have a mobile phone and a TV. ☐
2 Aled's mum said Aled couldn't stay at Danny's house. ☐
3 Aled had to be back before 11 o'clock. ☐
4 Aled and Danny went to the sports centre. ☐
5 Danny's cousin had some cider. ☐
6 Aled's dad was very angry when he saw Aled in Caernarfon. ☐

▸ S. 41

7 Finish Aled's e-mail to Steven, a friend in a different school. Use the words in the box.

alcohol • angry • cider • cousin
Friday • ~~grounded~~ • have to
mustn't • safe • strict • trouble

Hi Steven,
I'm *grounded* at the moment because my parents are very ____________ with me.

On ____________ I went to Caernarfon with Danny and his ____________ bought some ____________.

You know my parents are ____________ and say I ____________ drink any ____________.

Well, I thought I was ____________ in Caernarfon, but my dad saw me and I was in big ____________.

That's why I ____________ stay at home every weekend this month.
See you,
Aled

▸ S. 41

8 You're Aled. Write another e-mail to Steven and invite him for a weekend. Read the questions and look at the words in the boxes. They can help you.

When can Stephen come?	next weekend / next month / on …
What can you and Steven do when he's here?	blogging / mountain boarding / walking / eating / …
What do you want to ask Steven to bring?	warm clothes / computer games / mountain board / …

Hi Steven,

____

____

____

____

Bye, Aled

▸ S. 41

9 Parents! Finish the sentences with the right words.

1 Parents are often OK, but I think they are a *pain* when they always say 'No!'.

2 I go home from school by train, and my mum p__________ me up from the station.

3 My parents say I mustn't drink cider or any a__________.

4 My village is very, very boring. I can't do a__________ here!

5 I can never stay in town late. I can never go dancing. My mum is too s__________!

6 I want to go to school by bike, but my dad says cycling in town isn't s__________.

▸ S. 42

10 Aled is writing about his family. Circle the right words.

My family is from **Welsh/Wales**. *We live in the country and we have a small* **blogging/business** *– we hire* **mountain/moment** *bikes to tourists in spring, summer and* **aunt/autumn**. *I often* **interview/invite** *friends for a weekend, and then we* **ride/write** *the bikes too.*

▸ S. 42

11 Birthday presents. Finish the sentences with *this*, *that*, *these* or *those*.

I like __________ T-shirt there.

1

Hm, no, I think __________ green T-shirt is better for Jack.

__________ chocolates are too expensive!

2

Let's buy __________ chocolates there, then.

I think grandad likes __________ music.

3

Hm, I don't know. But I know he likes __________ songs.

Do you like __________ jeans over there?

4

No, they're terrible! But look at __________ bag. It's cool!

▸ S. 42

12 The year. Read the sentences. Write the words 1–6. Then write the missing word for 7 and tick the right answer for 8.

1 This is the first month of the year.
2 The name of the seventh month of the year.
3 It's often very cold in this season.
4 In this season the days are very long.
5 On this day many children get presents.
6 The month of April is in this season.

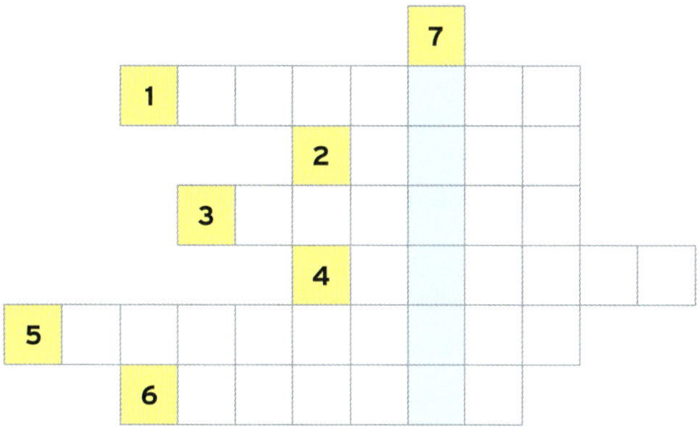

7 This word is ____________.

8 It's a … ☐ month. ☐ year. ☐ season. ☐ holiday.

▸ S. 43

13 What hobbies do people have? Write six sentences. The pictures and the words in the boxes can give you some ideas.

Many young people | Most people | Lots of people | People often | Some people

climb | collect | go | listen to
play | ride | watch | write

1 *Lots of people listen to music.*
2 ____________
3 ____________
4 ____________
5 ____________
6 ____________
7 ____________

▸ S. 43

14 LISTENING

New things. Tick the right phrase in a), then finish sentence b).

1 **a)** Adil asks about ☐ ringtones / ☐ text messages / ☐ text bullying.

b) Adil can't use the new phone because it doesn't have ______________________.

2 **a)** On Saturday Ben bought new ☐ jeans / ☐ trainers / ☐ DVDs.

b) He bought them in a shop near ____________________.

3 **a)** The new computer is in ☐ Ella's room / ☐ the living room / ☐ a box in the kitchen.

b) The name of the computer game is "__________________________________".

4 **a)** Tom's family bought a new car ☐ yesterday / ☐ this morning / ☐ last week.

b) Tom says the best thing about the car is that ____.

▸S. 44

15 SPEAKING

a) Look at the picture and answer the questions.

A Is that a new computer?

B Yes, ____________________________________ last week.

A It's ___________. Was it expensive?

B No, ____.

b) Choose one of the pictures.
Invent a dialogue with a partner.
Write it in your exercise book.
Then act the dialogue.

▸S. 45

● 16 INTERPRETING

You're in Wales with your parents.
You want to invite a Welsh girl, but she says she can't come.
Tell your parents what the girl is saying.

I'm in big trouble.
My parents are angry with
me because I drank alcohol
at a party. I'm grounded till
next month. My parents
are too strict!

Sie sagt, sie ____

Ihre Eltern ____

____

Sie ____

____

Sie findet, ____

▸S. 45

17 READING

a) Read the poem. Which title is best?

☐ My town ☐ Wales ☐ Seasons ☐ Friends

In summer ice cream is a treat
In autumn conkers in the street
In winter Christmas is the best
Spring flowers are nicer than all the rest.

Summer, autumn, winter, spring
There's a season for everything

Boring cricket in summer, hay fever and sneezing
In winter my fingers and toes are freezing
In autumn we have to go back to school
Clouds and spring showers – that just isn't cool!

Two children are playing conkers.

b) Words in the poem. Circle what these words are in German.

1 treat = *Genuss/Grauen*
2 the rest = *die anderen / die Ruhe*
3 cricket = *Krücken/Kricket*
4 hay fever = *Grippe/Heuschnupfen*
5 sneezing = *Niesen/Humpeln*
6 fingers and toes = *Finger und Zehen / Augen und Zähne*
7 are freezing = *braten/frieren*
8 showers = *Regen/Shows*

▸S. 47

18 WRITING

**a) Change the first part of the poem in exercise 17.
Use the words in the boxes or your own ideas.**

In summer ____________ a treat. | picnics/holidays/cycling/tennis/...

In autumn ____________ in the street. | playing football / riding my bike / jogging / ...

In winter ____________ is the best. | skiing/walking/reading/...

____________ nicer than all the rest. | Easter eggs / Christmas / birthday presents / ...

● **b) Change the words in red in the second part of the poem in exercise 17.
Here are some ideas. Write your poem in your exercise book.**

swimming/walking/lessons/...
my hands and feet are / my fish in the garden is / ...

Boring football in summer, ...
In winter ...

▸S. 47

CHECKPOINT

Die Hilfsverben *can/can't* und *have to / don't have to*

Trage hier den Checkpoint aus dem Schülerbuch (Seite 49) ein und schreibe deine eigenen Beispielsätze auf.

Mit __________ sagst du, was jemand tun kann oder darf.

Mit __________ sagst du, was jemand nicht tun kann oder nicht darf.

Mit __________ sagst du, was jemand tun muss.

Mit __________ sagst du, was jemand nicht zu tun braucht.

Meine Beispielsätze:

____

____

____

____

▸ S. 49

19 Deniz is talking about her school day. Finish the sentences with the words from the box.

can • can't • doesn't have to • don't have to • has to • have to (2x)

1 There's a bus to school, so I __________ walk.

2 But my bus is at 6.30 in the morning, so I __________ get up very early.

3 My sister goes to school by bike, so she __________ take the bus.

4 My sister's maths teacher can't hear very well, so my sister __________ shout.

5 I __________ eat at school because we have a good cafe there.

6 I __________ watch much TV because we always have lots of homework.

7 And sometimes I __________ help my dad in the kitchen.

▸ S. 49

20 **Read about school in Wales and then write about your school.**

At school in Wales	**At my school in** ______
1 The pupils have to wear a school uniform.	We ______ wear a school uniform.
2 They can't go home at 1 o'clock.	______
3 They have to go to school in the afternoon.	We ______ go to school in the afternoon.
4 They can have lunch at school.	______
5 They don't have to stand when another teacher comes into the classroom.	We ______ stand when another teacher comes into the classroom.
6 They can join clubs at school.	______

▸S. 49

21 **a) What about you? Finish the sentences with *can, can't, have to,* or *don't have to.***

1 I ______ go to school every day.
2 I ______ help at home every day.
3 I ______ play the guitar.
4 I ______ draw very well.
5 I ______ speak German.
6 I ______ speak another language.
7 I ______ get up very early.
8 I ______ go to bed very early.

b) Now answer these questions.

1 What sports can you play? – I ______.
2 What sport can't you play very well? – I ______.
3 What subjects do you have to learn at school? – We ______
______.
4 Do you have to learn Welsh? – No, we ______.

▸S. 49

TEST YOURSELF

1 Look at the picture. What's in this village?

There's ...

1 a ________________, 4 a ________________,

2 a ________________, 5 a ________________,

3 a ________________, 6 a ________________.

2 Circle the right word.

1 How much are *this/these* apples?

2 And how much are *those/these* bananas there?

3 Read the questions and write the answers.

1 Was this laptop expensive? – *No, / offer / it / on / was / special / .*

____

2 Do you like blogging? – *No, / a / of / waste / time / it's / .*

____

3 Is that a new bike? – *Yes, / last / Friday / it / I / bought / .*

____

4 Are you in trouble with your parents? – *Yes, / because / some / week / last / cider / I / bought / .*

____

4 What do teenagers think about their parents? Finish the sentences.

→ can • can't (2x) • don't have to have to (2x)

PARENTS – what our readers say

Parents are a pain when they say you (1) ________________ go to bed. But they're OK when they say you (2) ________________ help in the kitchen today!

Sam

Often I want to go into town with my friends, but my dad says I (3) __________ go before I do my homework. But I (4) __________ phone my friends from my room, so it's not so bad. *Amy*

I'm grounded this week, so I (5) __________ see my friends in the evening. I (6) __________ come home after school – it's terrible! I think my mum is too strict! *Alex*

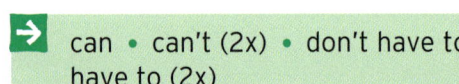

▸ Auf der Seite 70 findest du die Lösungen.

Unit 4

Northern lights

1 Photos of Blackpool. Look at the photos and write the right words.

1 ____________________

2 ____________________

3 ____________________

4 ____________________

5 ____________________

6 ____________________

7 ____________________

▸ S. 51

2 Listen again to the text about Blackpool. Are the sentences right (✓) or wrong (✗)?

1 Blackpool is in the south of England. ☐

2 It often rains in Blackpool. ☐

3 Blackpool has no amusement arcades. ☐

4 Blackpool Tower is like the Eiffel Tower, but smaller. ☐

5 There are no trams in Blackpool. ☐

6 Blackpool's funfair has a big roller coaster. ☐

Eiffel Tower

Blackpool Tower

▸ S. 50

3 What things use electricity in your school? Make a list. Find five things or more.

____

____

▸ S. 51

4 Read the article about Tim again. Finish the sentences.

→ buy some computer games • costs £50,000 • goes to the Blackpool Illuminations
has won £100 • uses lots of new technology • will be there with

1 Tim ______ in the Blackpool Illuminations quiz.

2 With the money he'll ______.

3 He ______ every year.

4 This year Tim ______ his dad and brother.

5 The show ______.

6 The electricity for the light show ______.

▸ S. 52

5 a) Write the numbers.

1 1,000,000 ______ 3 100 ______

2 1,000 ______ 4 1/2 ______

b) If you win in a quiz ... Find the right word.

1 You get this if you win in a quiz: ______

2 You say this to the winner: " ______ !"

3 Lots of lights: ______

4 You pay with it in Britain: ______

● **c) Explain the words.**

1 ______ : expensive 2 ______ : eye

▸ S. 52

6 How's Tim wasting energy? Put in the right words.

→ off (2x) • on (2x) • open • up

Tim's window is ______ and the radiator is ______. His charger is ______, but his phone is charged ______. Tim should turn ______ the charger and save energy. He should turn ______ the lights when he leaves the room too.

▸ S. 53

The dare

7 a) Read the sentences. Put them in the right order (1–9).

- [ ] Tim screamed, then he jumped into the sea. L
- [ ] Tim took off his jacket. P
- [ ] Tim was bored. B
- [ ] Tim and the other boys walked along the pier. C
- [ ] Tim and Dan climbed down the pier. O
- [ ] The gang met at the funfair. A
- [ ] Suddenly Dan wasn't there. O
- [ ] Leo said that Tim had to do a dare. K
- [ ] Dan invited Tim to join the gang. L

b) Where did the story happen? Use your answers and the letters in exercise 7a.

1	2	3	4	5	6	7	8	9

The story happened in ________________.

c) Which sentence in exercise 7a matches picture A / picture B?

A

Picture A =

sentence ___

B

Picture B =

sentence ___

d) Write the sentences from exercise 7a in the right order in your exercise book.

► S. 55

8 Sam and Adam come home very late and very wet. Their mother is angry. Finish Adam's answer with the words in the box. Write it in your exercise book.

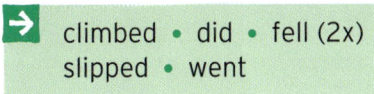

> climbed • did • fell (2x)
> slipped • went

ADAM

We're sorry, Mum. We .... a dare.
We ...... to Blackpool Pier.
We .... down the railing.
Sam's foot .... and he .... into the water. A minute later I .... too.

Sam! Adam! I was worried! Why are you so late and wet?

► S. 55

9 **a) At the funfair. Find the right words. Draw lines.**

1 The roller coaster is great – I love
2 If you go on the roller coaster, I'll go with
3 Mum is on it now – let's watch
4 Where's Dad? I can't find
5 He and Jamie are on the pier – can you see
6 We're going to the amusement arcade. Come with
7 I want to buy some chips first. Wait for

me.
you.
him.
her.
it!
us!
them?

b) Write the sentences in your exercise book.

▸ S. 56

10 **a) Circle the odd word out.**

eyes face hand jacket	brave frightened wet worried	bored climbed screamed slipped

● **b) Make three odd word out games for your partner.**

______ ______	______ ______	______ ______

▸ S. 56

11 **Bungee jumping in Blackpool. Put in the missing verbs.**

climbed • imagine • jumped • paid • screamed • thought • took • want • watch

Last summer I went bungee jumping in Blackpool – it was a dare! First, I ________ my money, then I ________ off my jacket and ________ onto the bridge. My friends ________ I was very brave, but you can ________ how nervous I felt! "________ me!" I shouted. Then I ________ from the bridge. Down, down I went. I ________, "Aaargh!" – but it was great! Now I ________ to go bungee jumping again!

bungee jumping

▸ S. 56

12 **a) A short talk. Read the sentences. Put them in the right order.**

☐ Secondly, it has his autograph on it too.

☐ So, to finish, I'd like to say that this photo is very important to me.

☐ I want to tell you about my photo of Wayne Rooney.

☐ Thirdly, it's special because he gave it to me.

☐ Firstly, I'm a big football fan.

b) Write the text in your exercise book.

c) Finish the notes from this short talk.

– *photo* ______________________

– *firstly: football* ______________________

– *secondly:* ______________________

– *thirdly:* ______________________

– *to finish:* ______________________

▸ S. 57

13 **a) You want to present a talk in class. Choose one of the following things. Write the talk in your exercise book. The notes can help you.**

- my new dog
- love animals
- it's a very sweet dog
- listens to me
- dog is important to me

- my mountain bike
- looks cool
- present from parents
- use it every day
- bike is important to me

b) Present the talk in your class.

▸ S. 57

SKILLS TRAINING

14 LISTENING

Match the photos with the instructions you hear. You don't need one of the photos.

A

instruction no. ______

B

instruction no. ______

C

instruction no. ______

D

instruction no. ______

► S. 58

15 INTERPRETING

You're in Blackpool. Your friend wants to buy a sandwich from a machine. A girl explains to you what to do. Tell your friend what to do in German.

GIRL First pick a sandwich and then press the red button.

YOU Sie sagt, du musst dir zuerst ______________________

und dann ______________________.

GIRL Then put the money in the machine.

YOU Dann musst du ______________________.

GIRL Now take your sandwich.

YOU Jetzt kannst du ______________________.

► S. 58

16 SPEAKING

a) Hakan wants to make lunch for Karen. Look at the picture and finish the dialogue.

HAKAN I'll make lunch. Would you like a sandwich?

KAREN Yes, ____________.

HAKAN ____________ or ____________?

KAREN ____________, please.

HAKAN What about a drink?

KAREN Yes, please. Do ______________________?

HAKAN ____________________.

KAREN ______________________ milk?

HAKAN Sure, no problem. I'll get it.

b) Invent a dialogue with a partner. Write it in your exercise book. Then act the dialogue.

► S. 59

17 READING

Read the brochure and answer the questions. Make notes.

Scarborough Sea Life Centre

Come and see our collection of thousands of beautiful fish and sea animals.

They live in the sea and have eight legs – visit our fantastic octopus exhibition.

Have fun with our interactive displays – they're great!

Find us by the sea in the North Bay.
Phone 01723 376125 and find out more.

Open every day (but not 24–26 December)
10 a.m.–5 p.m.

Tickets: adults £10.95, children £8.95

1 Is the Sea Life Centre open at Christmas? ______

2 What can you see there? ______

3 Where in Scarborough is the Sea Life Centre? ______

4 How much is it? ______

5 What's the telephone number? ______

▸ S. 61

18 WRITING

a) Whitby is a town in the north of England. Make a brochure for Whitby's museum, the *Dracula Experience*. Use the notes in the box. Exercise 17 can help you.

Information: models of Dracula • interactive displays • where: 9 Marine Parade
Tel. 01947 601923 • open: Mon–Sun 10 a.m.–9 p.m. • adults: £1.95, children: £1.50

WHITBY DRACULA EXPERIENCE

Come and see our ______

______

______

______

______

______

b) Find information about another tourist place in Britain, and make a brochure for it.

▸ S. 61

CHECKPOINT

Will ('ll)* und *won't

Trage hier den Checkpoint aus dem Schülerbuch (Seite 63) ein und schreibe deine eigenen Beispielsätze auf.

Wenn du voraussagen willst, was ______________________________,

benutzt du ________ oder ______.

Beispiele: ______________________________

Wenn du voraussagen willst, was in der Zukunft *nicht* geschehen wird, benutzt du

________.

Beispiele: ______________________________

Fragen mit *will* werden durch die ______________ angezeigt.

Beispiele: ______________________________

▸ S. 63

19 a) Make a brochure about a trip to Blackpool. Look at the pictures. Write six sentences for the brochure in your exercise book. The words in the box can help you.

Saturday morning	Saturday afternoon	Saturday evening	Sunday morning	Sunday afternoon	Sunday evening

eat	the funfair
play	fish and chips
look at	in the sea
see	Blackpool Tower
swim	the illuminations
go to	electronic games at the amusement arcade

On Saturday morning you'll see Blackpool Tower.
In the afternoon you'll ...

b) Write two more sentences for the brochure. Invent the activities.

____

____

▸ S. 63

20 **Sam and Amy want to go to Blackpool next weekend. Write their questions and answers about the trip.**

1 SAM we / the / go / to / beach? / Will
Will we go to the beach?

2 AMY Yes, / raining. / but / won't / if / we / it's / go

3 SAM Blackpool Pier? / will / we / to / When / go

4 AMY go / We'll / Saturday. / on / there

5 SAM fun? / the / Will / trip / be

6 AMY the / be / interesting. / trip / Yes, / very / will

7 SAM I / I'll / think / with / friend / my / bring / me.

8 AMY That's OK. But please don't bring your dog ...

▸S. 63

21 **a) What do you think will happen in your future?**

1 Will you have children? (If yes, how many?)

I think I

2 Where will you live?

3 Will people save more energy?

4 Will the weather be warmer?

5 Will people live on Mars?

b) Write two more things that you think will/won't happen in your future. Use the words in the box or your own ideas.

good job / pets
famous / go on a trip / ...

▸S. 63

TEST YOURSELF

1 **Sarah is writing an e-mail to her best friend Rebecca. Finish the sentences.**

→ him • it • me • them • us

Hi Rebecca,
My parents gave ________ an MP3 player for my birthday. I listen to ________ every day.

I usually listen to Robbie Williams – I love ________! I have all his CDs – you can borrow ________.

Mum and I are going to see Robbie Williams in May. You could come with ________!
Love, Sarah

2 **Match the words.**

amusement • charged • ~~DVD~~ internet • roller • take

arcade • coaster • kiosk off • ~~player~~ • up

1 *DVD player* 2 ________ 3 ________

4 ________ 5 ________ 6 ________

3 **Tim, your British friend, is staying with you. Your mum wants to make lunch for him. Tell your mum in German what Tim is saying to her.**

MUM Möchtest du ein Sandwich, Tim? **TIM** Yes, please – I'm hungry.

YOU Tim sagt ________ – er ________

MUM Mit Käse oder mit Huhn? **TIM** Cheese, please.

YOU Er sagt, er hätte gern ein Brot mit ________

MUM Und etwas zu trinken? **TIM** Do you have milk?

YOU Er fragt, ________

4 **Finish the sentences. Use the words in the boxes.**

'll • won't + buy • find • make • ~~open~~ turn off • close • waste

1 I'm hot! – OK, I'll *open* the window.

2 I'm cold! – OK, ________ the window.

3 The TV is on, but we aren't watching it. – OK, ________ the TV so we ________ energy.

4 Where's my mobile phone? – I ________ it for you.

5 Oh no – we don't have any cola! – OK, OK. I ________ some cola at the shop.

6 I'm hungry! Will you make lunch? – No, I ________ lunch! You can do it!

▸ Die Lösungen findest du auf Seite 71.

Hier kannst du darüber nachdenken, was du in den Units 3 und 4 schon alles gelernt hast.

Das kann ich!

Male die Kästchen aus. Leer bedeutet „das muss ich noch üben" ☐, halb ausgemalt bedeutet „das kann ich mit Hilfe" ☐ und vollständig ausgemalt bedeutet „das kann ich bereits gut" ☐.

Unit 3

Ich kann in vier Sätzen sagen, welche Freizeitaktivitäten ich mag / nicht mag.
(Tipp: Schau dir die Übung 5 auf Seite 26 an.) ☐

Ich kann Sätze mit *this, that, these* und *those* bilden.
(Tipp: Schau dir die Übung 11 auf Seite 28 an.) ☐

Ich kann in drei Sätzen etwas über Handys, MP3-Player oder andere technische Geräte sagen.
(Tipp: Schau dir die Übung 15 auf Seite 30 an.) ☐

Ich kann zwei Sätze mit *can* und zwei Sätze mit *can't* bilden.
(Tipp: Schau dir die Übungen 19–21 auf den Seiten 32–33 an.) ☐

Ich kann zwei Sätze mit *have to / has to* und zwei Sätze mit *don't have to / doesn't have to* bilden.
(Tipp: Schau dir die Übungen 19–21 auf den Seiten 32–33 an.) ☐

Der Titel meiner Arbeit für das Portfolio lautet:

____

Unit 4

Ich kann vier Sätze mit *me, you, him, her, it, us* oder *them* bilden.
(Tipp: Schau dir die Übung 9 auf Seite 38 an.) ☐

Ich kann in fünf Sätzen über Personen, Tiere oder Dinge sprechen, die mir wichtig sind, z. B. *My favourite football player ..., My dog ...*
(Tipp: Schau dir die Übung 13 auf Seite 39 an.) ☐

Ich kann in vier Sätzen beschreiben, wie man einen Getränkeautomaten bedient, z. B. *Put a pound in the machine.*
(Tipp: Schau dir die Übung 15 auf Seite 40 an.) ☐

Ich kann etwas zu essen und zu trinken anbieten, z. B. *Would you like ...?*
(Tipp: Schau dir die Übung 16 auf Seite 40 an.) ☐

Ich kann vier Sätze darüber bilden, was in der Zukunft geschehen wird oder nicht geschehen wird, z. B. *I think I'll have three children.*
(Tipp: Schau dir die Übungen 20–21 auf Seite 43 an.) ☐

Der Titel meiner Arbeit für das Portfolio lautet:

____

Tipp: Du kannst auch deine Lehrerin / deinen Lehrer fragen, welche Fortschritte du im Englischunterricht gemacht hast.

PORTFOLIO

Das kann ich auch noch!

Ich kann die zwölf Monate auf Englisch nennen.
(Tipp: Schau dir Seite 43 im Schülerbuch an.)

Ich kenne fünf Wörter, mit denen ich Gefühle beschreiben kann, z. B. *angry*.
(Tipp: Schau dir Seite 28 im Schülerbuch an.)

So lerne ich Englisch!

Was findest du beim Englischlernen am einfachsten? Was kommt dir schwieriger vor?
Ergänze ein Smiley für jede Aussage:

☺ = normalerweise einfach; 😐 = manchmal einfach; ☹ = hier brauche ich noch Übung.

Ich kann ...	
... meinen Lehrer / meine Lehrerin verstehen, wenn er/sie Englisch spricht.	
... Hörtexte auf einer CD verstehen.	
... mir gut neue Wörter merken.	
... mit einem Partner / einer Partnerin einen Dialog vorbereiten.	
... auf Englisch Notizen zu einem Thema machen.	
... die Bedeutung neuer Wörter in einem Text herausfinden.	

Lerntipp

Wenn ..., dann ... Diese Tipps sollen dir beim Verstehen von neuen Texten weiterhelfen.
Kannst du die Satzteile so zusammenfügen, dass sinnvolle Ratschläge entstehen?

... lese ich sie mir gründlich durch, weil sie mir Hinweise geben, worum es im Text geht. • ... in Panik auszubrechen, weil dies ganz normal ist. • ... sie im *dictionary* nachzuschlagen. • ... lese ich den Text noch einmal durch. • ... schaue ich es mir zuerst an, da es mir etwas über den Text verraten kann.

- Wenn es ein Bild zum Text gibt, ____________________
- Wenn es eine Überschrift oder Anweisungen zum Text gibt, ____________________
- Wenn ich nicht jedes Wort verstehe, ist es nicht nötig, ____________________
- Wenn ich wichtige Wörter auch aus dem Zusammenhang nicht verstehe, ist es hilfreich, ____________________
- Wenn ich alle wichtigen Vokabeln geklärt habe, ____________________

Unit 5

Dubliners

1 Listen again and tick (✓) the right phrase.

1 Liam goes to the athletics club ...

every day. ☐ every week. ☐ every month. ☐

2 Tess is ...

his sister. ☐ his dog. ☐ his mother. ☐

3 Liam was at the sea in Howth ...

last February. ☐ last weekend. ☐ last summer. ☐

▸ S. 64

2 A family quiz. Write the right words.

1 My father's sister is my *aunt*.

2 My mother's mother is my ______________.

3 My sister is my mother's ______________.

4 My mother's father is my ______________.

5 My aunt's daughter is my ______________.

6 My mum and dad are my ______________.

▸ S. 64

3 Look at the pictures. Then write the sentences with the words in the right order.

1 me / this / family / with / is / my / .
see / can / you / right / me / on / the / .

This ______________________________

____

2 often / mountains / we / to / go / the / .
to / in / the / country / be / my / loves / dog / .

We ______________________________

____

3 at / centre / week / I / sports / every / the / train / .
go / my / with / friends / I / always / there / .

____

____

▸ S. 65

4 What do you remember about Liam and Gina? Finish the sentences.

the others will help | he'll buy a cool car | she'll get a good job | he'll be very happy | the Wards will buy a house

1 If Liam comes first in the Dublin Games, ______________________________.

2 If Liam gets a good job, ______________________________.

3 If one of the travellers has a problem, ______________________________.

4 If Gina's dad gets a job, ______________________________.

5 If Gina finishes school, ______________________________.

▸ S. 66

5 Small but important words. Finish the sentences about Liam.

Liam O'Brien lives ________ Dublin ________ his mum and his sister. Liam thinks that friends are ________ important. They helped him ________ when he had a difficult time two years ________. What are Liam's dreams ________ the future? He hopes ________ he'll find a nice girlfriend. He wants ________ get a good job. And he also wants ________ travel ________ lots ________ places.

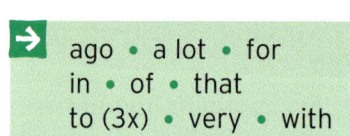

→ ago • a lot • for
in • of • that
to (3x) • very • with

▸ S. 66

6 a) And you? What do you hope for next weekend? Write four sentences.

I / my best friend / my parents / my sister / we / …	will/'ll won't	finish/go/have/ meet/play/watch/ …	TV/ football/ friends/…

1 I hope *I'll* ______________________________

2 I hope ______________________________

3 I hope ______________________________

4 And I hope ______________________________

● **b) Write four more sentences in your exercise book.**

▸ S. 67

Two worlds?

7 **Read and answer the questions. Start in the yellow box.**
- **If your answer is red, follow the red line to the next question.**
- **If your answer is green, follow the green line to the next question.**
- **If you follow the right lines, the nine black letters will tell you what Liam and Gina are.**

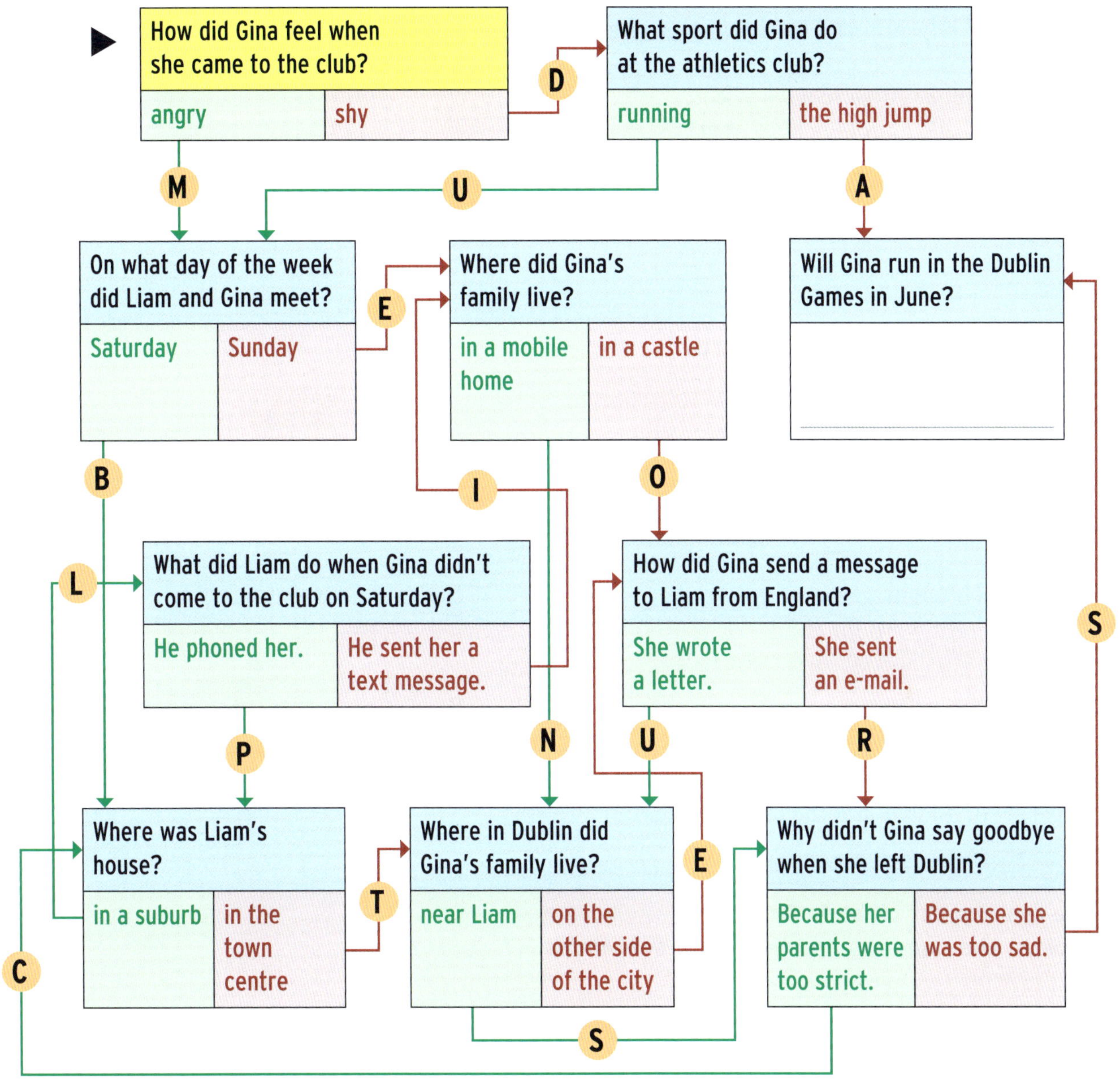

Liam and Gina are ☐☐☐☐☐☐☐☐☐.

▸ S. 69

8 **Write Liam's e-mail to Gina in your exercise book.**
Tell her how you felt when you found out that she was in England.
Invite her for June:
– say she can stay in your house and
– say what you can do together.

Hi Gina!
I was really happy when I got …
When you didn't come to the club, I …
It's great that you can … in June. You can stay at …
We can … or maybe we can … I'm sure we … fun.
And I hope I … in the Dublin Games.
Love, …

▸ S. 69

9 **How do they feel? Write sentences about Sarah, David, Tom and Mrs Parks. You'll only need four of the words in the box.**

beautiful • busy • devastated • famous • fast • ill • shy • strict

I'm in bed today. I don't feel OK. SARAH

It's terrible. My girlfriend has left me. DAVID

I'd like to invite Anna to my house. Can I ask her? I don't know ... TOM

Look at your book! Don't talk with your partner! MRS PARKS

1 Sarah is ______________.

2 David ______________.

3 ______________

4 ______________

▸ S. 70

10 **Write the words in the crossword.**

Across →

1 There are eleven players in a football ...
4 In winter you play sports indoors in a ...
6 Roisdorf is a village; Bonn is a big ...
8 Chairs, tables, beds and cupboards.
9 Athletics are sports like ... or high jump.
10 You do it when you're hungry.
11 A different word for child.

Down ↓

2 You can stay ... my house.
3 ..., afternoon, evening.
5 Gina left Dublin and ... back to England.
7 A part of a town, not the town centre.

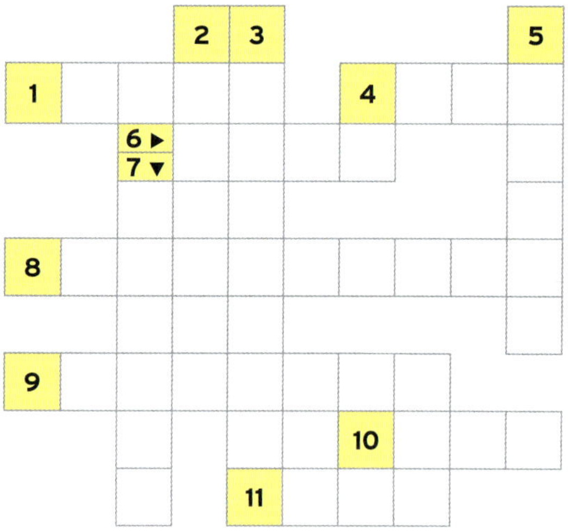

▸ S. 70

11 **The ten biggest cities in Britain. Look at the numbers and finish the sentences.**

	Cities	People
1	London	7,172,091
2	Birmingham	970,892
3	Glasgow	629,501
4	Liverpool	469,017
5	Leeds	443,247
6	Sheffield	439,866
7	Edinburgh	430,082
8	Bristol	420,556
9	Manchester	394,269
10	Leicester	330,574

1 The fourth biggest town is ______________.

2 Birmingham is the ______________ biggest town.

3 The ______________ biggest town is Sheffield.

4 ______________ is the eighth biggest town.

5 Glasgow is the ______________ biggest town.

6 The ______________ biggest town is Leeds.

▸ S. 70

12 a) Which of these words are people? Tick (✔) the boxes.

blogger ☐ cider ☐ driver ☐ farmer ☐ gardener ☐
hairdresser ☐ hamburger ☐ helper ☐ jogger ☐ order ☐
quarter ☐ remember ☐ shopper ☐ singer ☐ summer ☐
teenager ☐ together ☐ worker ☐

b) Finish the sentences about people.

1 People who play football are football ______________.

2 My sister is a good ______________. She swims in her school team.

3 A ______________ is somebody who writes books or stories.

4 Cindy wants to become a ______________. She likes singing.

5 ______________ like travelling, they don't stay for long in the same place.

Gardeners are people who work in gardens.

▸ S. 71

13 a) Tom is writing an e-mail to his German friend Leon. Finish the sentences.

→ get • get up • got • had • has • live • have (2x) • work

Hi Leon!
Thanks for your postcard – I ________ it this morning.
I really like basketball too, but I ________ no time for training because
I have a weekend job in a shop. The shop is in town, but I ________ in the
country, so I have to ________ early and I ________ no breakfast
because I'm usually late. And then I have to ________ hard in the shop!
My friend Jack ________ a party last Saturday, but I was too tired!
But if my school ________ a match soon, I hope I'll ________ on the team!
Best wishes, Tom

● **b) INTERPRETING**

Your friend Leon can't understand the e-mail from his friend Tom.
Write the e-mail in German in your exercise book. *Du kannst deinen Text auf ein Blatt Papier schreiben und es dann am linken Rand dieser Seite festkleben.*

▸ S. 71

14 LISTENING

a) Look at the pictures. Then listen to dialogue 1. Tick (✓) the right pictures A or B.

1 This afternoon …

A

B

2 Last week …

A

B

b) Listen to dialogue 2. Tick (✓) the words which you hear.

homework ☐ hour ☐ strict ☐ teacher ☐ lesson ☐ school ☐

c) Listen to dialogue 3. Finish the sentences.

Sarah and Ines will meet in the teachers' ________ at ________________.

Ines: The best place for presents is the ________________ behind the ________________.

Sarah: The best place for presents are the ________________ near the ________________.

► S. 72

15 SPEAKING

a) Jack and Tim are talking at the end of the school day. Tick the right answer.

1 JACK Hi, Tim. Geography was really good today, wasn't it?
TIM **a)** I agree. But it isn't always like that! ☐
b) I don't agree! It was really good. ☐

2 JACK But we have too much maths homework!
TIM **a)** That's true. We should have more homework. ☐
b) You're right. We should tell our teacher. ☐

3 JACK And we write too many tests.
TIM **a)** That isn't true. We wrote only two tests last year. ☐
b) I don't think you're right. We wrote lots of tests. ☐

b) Invent a dialogue with your partner. The words in the box can help you. Never agree with your partner! Write the dialogue in your exercise book. Then act the dialogue.

A Football is boring!
B Oh, I don't agree! Football is great!
A But I think running is easy!
B That isn't true! Running is …

school subjects: music, history, …
sports: running, high jump, …
free time: carnival, funfairs, roller coasters, amusement arcades, …

what you think: interesting, easy, great, really good, hard, funny, exciting, dangerous, silly, terrible, …

► S. 73

16 READING

a) Underline in the text …

1 in green: five places in the country,
2 in red: six animals,
3 in yellow: six things in a hotel room,
4 in blue: five activities.

b) Which sentences are right (✔)? Which sentences are wrong (✘)?

1 The hotel is on a cliff. ☐
2 You can eat in the restaurant at half past nine in the evening. ☐
3 You can bring dogs to the hotel. ☐

Dingle Hotel, Ireland

If you like green fields with sheep and cows in them, mountains, and rivers with lots of fish, this is the hotel for you. Standing next to the beach, the hotel is ideal for walking, fishing, swimming and golf. Take a boat trip on the sea, and you'll see hundreds of birds on the cliffs, and you'll maybe see whales too.

Our hotel is famous for its beautiful furniture in every room. All our rooms have fine beds, colour TV, mini-bar, telephone – and good hot radiators if you come in winter!
Our restaurant is open 6 p.m.–9 p.m.
Quiet dogs are welcome in the hotel.

▸S. 74

17 WRITING

A holiday in Northern Ireland. Look at the pictures and do exercises a), b) and c). Write the story in your exercise book.

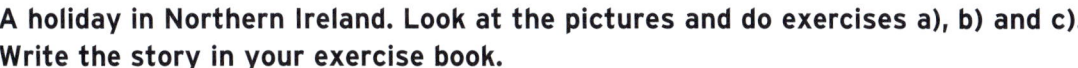

a) Put the red words in the right order.

(weeks/ago/two) Mrs Beck, Julia and Holger *(Belfast/to/travelled)*. When they *(airport/at/Belfast/arrived)*, their friend David met them. *"Belfast/welcome/to"*, he said. Then *(drove/house/David's/to/they)*.

b) Write the verbs in the simple past.

The next day David *(go)* into town with the Becks. They *(see)* lots of places and David *(talk)* a lot. Mrs Beck *(listen)* to him and Julia *(take)* lots of photos. But Holger only *(send)* text messages to his friends.

● **c) Answer the questions.**

– What did they do in the evening?
– What did they see?
– What did they hear?
– What did they eat?
– How did Mrs Beck feel?

▸S. 75

CHECKPOINT

_If_-Sätze
Trage hier den Checkpoint aus dem Schülerbuch (Seite 77) ein und schreibe deine eigenen Beispielsätze auf.

Nebensatz	Hauptsatz
	______________
If + ______________	______________ + verb
	______________

Meine Beispielsätze:

If ______________________________

____

▸ S. 77

18 Look at the tips from Ellington Health Centre. Make sentences. Draw lines.

ELLINGTON HEALTH CENTRE
If you want the good life – read our tips!

1 If you eat fruit and vegetables every day,	you should wear a helmet.
2 If your older brothers and sisters drive a car,	you should wear safety gear.
3 If skaters and snowboarders aren't careful,	they shouldn't drink alcohol.
4 If you ride a motorbike,	it won't be dangerous.
5 If you train your dog well,	they can slip and fall.
6 If you do dangerous sports,	you won't be ill so often.

▸ S. 77

19 Plans for the weekend. Circle the right words.

1 If *it's* / *it'll be* sunny on Saturday, we'll work in the garden.
2 But if you get on the rugby team, of course *we'll come* / *we come* and watch your match.
3 If your team *wins* / *'ll win*, we'll eat in a good restaurant in town.
4 Of course, if we stay too long, *we can't go* / *we go* to the cinema.
5 Then, if we're tired on Sunday, *we go* / *we won't go* out.
6 And if there's a good film on TV, *we can watch* / *we watch* it.

▸ S. 77

20 **Finish the sentences. Use the words in the boxes or your own ideas. Then sit in a group of four and read your sentences. Who has the funniest sentences?**

1 no chocolate / no DVDs / no crisps / ...

If our shop has ______________________________,

I'll be devastated!

2 do homework / find flip phone / clean my room / ...

If you ______________________________

______________ next week, I'll always be your friend!

3 smile/win/buy/...

If ______________________________

______________, I'll be the happiest teenager in the world!

4 get / have to / rain / ...

If ______________________________

______________________, I'll be very sad.

► S. 77

● **21** **Answer the questions about next weekend. Start with the underlined part.**

1 What will you do <u>if the weather is good</u>?

If the weather is good, I'll ______________________________

2 What will you do <u>if it rains</u>?

If ______________________________

3 What will you do in the evening <u>if there are no good films on TV</u>?

If ______________________________

4 When will you get up on Sunday <u>if you're very tired</u>?

If I'm ______________________________

► S. 77

TEST YOURSELF

1 Write the words.

1 Another word for children is ______________.

2 Now it's July. Two months ______________ it was May.

3 Two examples of athletics are ______________ and ______________.

4 Beds and tables are examples of ______________.

5 A ______________ road is a road with lots of cars.

6 This country has four parts: England, Scotland, ______________ and ______________.

2 Liam's lessons on Monday. Finish the sentences. Write words, not numbers.

1 His *last* lesson on Monday is art.

2 His ______________ lesson is English.

3 His ______________ lesson is history.

4 His ______________ lesson is maths.

5 His ______________ lesson is music.

3 Find the partners. You won't need all the words in the box.

> great • I hugged him. • It isn't hard. • really bad • really shy
> That's wrong. • ~~You're right.~~ • You're welcome.

1 I agree. *You're right.*

2 I'm happy that you're here. ______________

3 terrible ______________

4 That isn't true. ______________

5 I have no problem with it. ______________

6 fine ______________

4 Write the sentences with the words in the right order.

1 friend / If / Spain / my / back / to / moves / devastated. / 'll / I / be

____

2 I / third / If / come / the / competition / in / worry. / I / won't

____

▸ Die Lösungen findest du auf den Seiten 71–72.

Hier kannst du darüber nachdenken, was du in Unit 5 schon alles gelernt hast.

Das kann ich!

Male die Kästchen aus. Leer bedeutet „das muss ich noch üben" ☐, halb ausgemalt bedeutet „das kann ich mit Hilfe" ◧ und vollständig ausgemalt bedeutet „das kann ich bereits gut" ■.

Unit 5

Ich kann in vier Sätzen über meine Hoffnungen sprechen, z. B. *I hope I'll have lots of money.* ☐
(Tipp: Schau dir die Übung 6 auf Seite 48 an.)

Ich kann auf drei verschiedene Weisen Zustimmung ausdrücken und auf drei verschiedene Weisen etwas ablehnen, z. B. *You're right!* ☐
(Tipp: Schau dir die Übung 15 auf Seite 52 an.)

Ich kann mit Hilfen eine kurze Bildgeschichte schreiben. ☐
(Tipp: Schau dir die Übung 17 auf Seite 53 an.)

Ich kann vier Sätze mit *if* bilden. ☐
(Tipp: Schau dir die Übungen 18–21 auf den Seiten 54–55 an.)

Der Titel meiner Arbeit für das Portfolio lautet:

____

Das kann ich auch noch!

Ich kann Verben in Nomen verwandeln, z. B. *train – trainer; blog – blogger.* ☐
(Tipp: Schau dir Seite 71 im Schülerbuch an.)

Quiz

What do you know about Britain and Ireland? Tick the right answers.

- UNIT 1: The place in the photo is ...
  ☐ the Millennium Bridge. ☐ the London Eye. ☐ Big Ben.
- UNIT 2: Scotland is part of ...
  ☐ Ireland. ☐ England. ☐ Britain.
- UNIT 3: In Wales, they speak English and ...
  ☐ French. ☐ Welsh. ☐ Gaelic.
- UNIT 4: Blackpool is in the ...
  ☐ north ☐ south ☐ centre of England.
- UNIT 5: Dublin is in ...
  ☐ Wales. ☐ Ireland. ☐ Scotland.

Tipp: Du kannst auch deine Lehrerin / deinen Lehrer fragen, welche Fortschritte du im Englischunterricht gemacht hast.

PORTFOLIO

Hier kannst du darüber nachdenken, was du in Unit 6 schon alles gelernt hast.

Das kann ich!

Male die Kästchen aus. Leer bedeutet „das muss ich noch üben" ☐, halb ausgemalt bedeutet „das kann ich mit Hilfe" ◧ und vollständig ausgemalt bedeutet „das kann ich bereits gut" ■.

Unit 6

Ich kann einige deutsche Wörter, deren Übersetzung ich nicht kenne, auf Englisch umschreiben, z. B. *Geschirrspülmaschine, Handtuch, ...* ☐
(Tipp: Schau dir die Übungen 14–15 auf Seite 63 an.)

Ich kann beim Einkaufen vom Deutschen ins Englische dolmetschen. ☐
(Tipp: Schau dir die Übung 16 auf Seite 63 an.)

Ich kann eine E-Mail schreiben, in der ich in fünf Sätzen meine Urlaubserlebnisse schildere. ☐
(Tipp: Schau dir die Übung 20 auf Seite 65 an.)

Ich kann zwei Sätze mit *before* und zwei Sätze mit *after* bilden und dabei von Handlungen in der Vergangenheit berichten. ☐
(Tipp: Schau dir die Übungen 21–24 auf den Seiten 66–67 an.)

Der Titel meiner Arbeit für das Portfolio lautet:

____

Das kann ich auch noch!

Ich kann in einem Restaurant/Café etwas bestellen oder nach etwas fragen. z. B. *Can I have ..., please?* ☐
(Tipp: Schau dir Seite 84 im Schülerbuch an.)

Ready for *New Highlight 4*!

Band 3 von *New Highlight* hast du fast geschafft. Toll! Ein guter Zeitpunkt, um einmal aufzuschreiben, was dir **a)** in Englisch besonders gefällt, **b)** dir schon gut gelingt und **c)** was deine Ziele im nächsten Jahr sein könnten.

englische Texte lesen | mit einem Partner arbeiten | Gespräche auf Englisch führen | in einer Gruppe arbeiten | englische Hörtexte auf einer CD verstehen | Texte schreiben

a) ______________________________

b) ______________________________

c) ______________________________

Tipp: Du kannst auch deine Lehrerin / deinen Lehrer fragen, welche Fortschritte du im Englischunterricht gemacht hast.

Unit 6*

Cornish holidays

1 Listen again to the three dialogues. Tick (✓) the right answers.

1 The girl wants ... ☐ a white T-shirt. ☐ a blue T-shirt. ☐ a pink T-shirt.

2 The man got his tattoos in ... ☐ New York. ☐ London. ☐ Newquay.

3 In Florida the water is ... ☐ warmer ☐ cleaner ☐ colder
than in Cornwall.

4 The girl wants to buy ... ☐ a postcard. ☐ a poster. ☐ a picture.

▸S. 79

2 What are these hobbies? Write the words.

1 **cmpng**
camping

2 **snbthng**
____

3 **slng**
____

4 **pntng**
____

5 **fshng**
____

6 **wndsrfng**
____

▸S. 79

3 Find seven words and write them in the right box.

☺ I like it – I think it's ...

fun, __________

____

☹ I don't like it – I think it's ...

____

____

W	O	I	P	U	F	W	Q	C	E
D	X	N	C	X	V	U	Z	S	R
I	K	T	C	O	N	G	N	W	B
S	P	E	Q	V	O	T	J	L	O
T	E	R	R	I	B	L	E	T	R
U	Z	E	E	C	O	V	B	E	I
P	E	S	I	S	R	W	J	U	N
I	Y	T	O	F	I	P	F	R	G
D	H	I	L	A	N	L	K	N	L
B	M	N	X	Q	G	Z	L	S	J
S	D	G	R	E	A	T	M	Y	P

▸S. 79

4 Write about four hobbies you like and four hobbies you don't like in your exercise book. Say why. You can use the words you found in exercise 3.

I don't like jogging.
I think it's very boring and a waste of time!

▸S. 79

* Unit 6 ist nur Pflichtstoff für den E-Kurs in Nordrhein-Westfalen.

5 **Read the dialogue again. Then answer the questions.**

1 Is Matt working in his own cafe?

No, he's working ______________________________

2 Why's Matt working there today?

____

3 What does Matt's mum think of his clothes?

____

4 Why doesn't Matt's mum like Matt's hair?

____

5 What does Matt want to do on Saturday afternoon?

____

6 What must Matt do in the morning?

____

▸S. 80

6 **a) Cornish pasties. Put the instructions in the right order.**

☐	Bake the pasties at 220° C.
☐	Cut the pastry round a small plate.
1	Make the pastry.
☐	Cut and mix the beef and vegetables.
☐	Roll out the pastry.
☐	Put the beef and vegetables on the pastry and make pasties.

b) Write the right sentence for picture A.

____

▸S. 81

7  **Write six sentences or more about your favourite cafe/restaurant in your exercise book.**

- What's it like?
- What's in the cafe/restaurant?
- What can you eat and drink there?

My favourite cafe/restaurant is ...
It's ...
There's ...
There are ...
You can eat/drink ...

▸S. 81

Too young

8 Who ...? Read the story again and then answer these questions.

1 Who was busy in the cafe on Saturday? ______________________

2 Who looked bored? ______________________

3 Who were fans of *Lemon Jelly*? ______________________

4 Who painted pictures with Matt? ______________________

5 Who bought Matt's and Jake's pictures? ______________________

6 Who wanted a tattoo? ______________________

▸S. 83

9 Finish the story with words from the box.

beach party • busy • expensive • gone • menu
money • painted • self-service • tattoo • young

Matt was very ______________ in the cafe. A German family was waiting with the ______________, so Matt told them that the cafe was ______________. Later, Matt wanted to invite the boy to a ______________, but the family had ______________. Matt and his friend Jake ______________ pictures, and made ______________ from tourists. They were in the street when they saw the boy and girl again. The girl wanted to have a ______________. She said it was too ______________ but really, she was too ______________.

▸S. 83

10 You meet a British girl/boy at a beach party. Write a dialogue in your exercise book. Make five sentences or more.

You: Hi, I'm Marlene. What's your name?
Partner: I'm Ann. Where are you from, Marlene?

hobbies?
school?
brothers and sisters?
age?
music?
your town?

▸S. 83

WORDPOWER

11 **a) Finish the networks.**

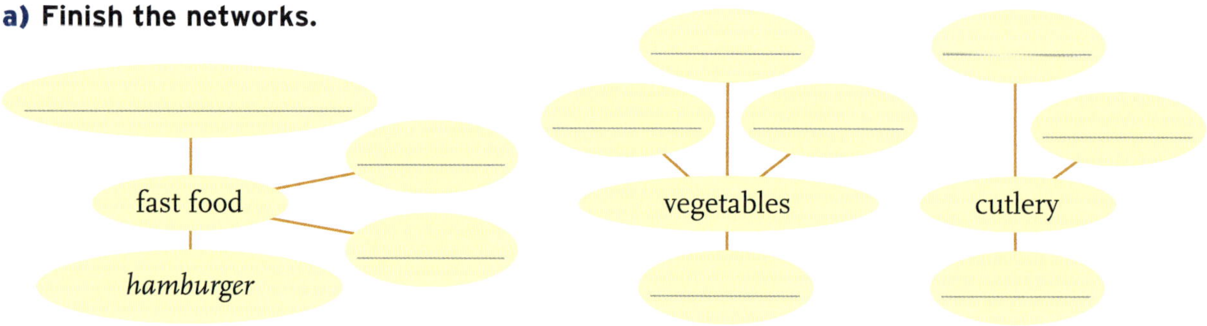

b) Make two networks in your exercise book: 1) fruits; 2) places where you find food.

▸ S. 84

12 **Write the right verbs.**

bake ______________ ______________

______________ ______________ ______________

▸ S. 84

13 **A tourist in England. Write the words in the right order.**

1 mean / ? / that / does / what

2 that / . / didn't / understand / I

3 she / ? / did / what / say

4 again, / can / say / ? / you / please / that

5 England / my / trip / to / first / . / is / this

▸ S. 84

14 What is it?

→ a menu • cutlery • a mirror • a plate • a tattoo • a pasty

1 You use it to eat food.

______

2 It's a kind of food from Cornwall.

______

3 It's a thing where you can see yourself.

______

4 It's a list of food in a cafe.

______

5 It's a kind of picture you can have on your arm.

______

6 You put food onto this.

______

▸ S. 85

15 Explain these words in English.

1 *Kohl* ______

2 *Spezi* ______

3 *Kleiderschrank* ______

______

4 *Badeanzug* ______

▸ S. 85

16 INTERPRETING

You're shopping with your German friend, Leonie, in Cornwall.
She doesn't know much English. Explain in English what your friend says.

LEONIE	*Ich würde gern das grüne T-Shirt da drüben anprobieren.*	YOU	My friend would like to ______
SHOP ASSISTANT	No problem. What size does she take?	YOU	*Welche Größe hast du, Leonie?*
LEONIE	*Ich habe Größe 38.*	YOU	______
SHOP ASSISTANT	OK, here you are.		
LEONIE	*Wo ist die Umkleidekabine?*	YOU	______
SHOP ASSISTANT	It's at the back of the shop.	YOU	*Sie ist hinten im Laden.*
LEONIE	*Frag mal, ob sie Badeschuhe oder andere Schuhe haben.*	YOU	______
SHOP ASSISTANT	No, sorry, we don't sell shoes.	YOU	*Nein, sie verkaufen keine Schuhe.*
LEONIE	*OK. Danke schön.*	YOU	______

▸ S. 85

17 LISTENING

A survey with tourists. Listen and make notes.

Newquay Tourist Survey	Dialogue 1	Dialogue 2
1 Where are they from?		
2 How long are they staying?		
3 Where are they staying?		
4 What do they like in Newquay?		

Newquay Tourist Survey	Dialogue 3	Dialogue 4
1 Where are they from?		
2 How long are they staying?		
3 Where are they staying?		
4 What do they like in Newquay?		

▸ S. 86

18 SPEAKING

a) Helping visitors. Write the dialogue in the right order in your exercise book.

Thanks. And where can I buy some apples?

You're welcome.

There's a supermarket in King Street. It's opposite the station.

It's in Cromwell Street, near the park. You can't miss it.

Thank you.

Excuse me, where's the tourist office, please?

b) Invent a dialogue with your partner. Change the red words in exercise 18a. The pictures can give you some ideas. Write your dialogue in your exercise book. Then act the dialogue.

▸ S. 87

19 READING

Read the text.

Disaster in Boscastle

The village of Boscastle, in the north of Cornwall, has always been popular with tourists. They come to look at the fishing boats in the small harbour, and visit the interesting old churches. They walk by the three rivers and go to the Museum of Witchcraft, next to the harbour.

A beautiful tourist village … But in 2004, disaster came to Boscastle: on the 16th August, there was terrible weather and a sudden flood. There was water everywhere. The flood badly damaged many houses, shops and the museum. The water pushed more than 100 cars into the harbour. All night boats helped to take people from their houses. Fortunately, nobody died.

Now the tourists are back in Boscastle. But the village won't forget that terrible August night in 2004.

a) What's the text about? Tick the right answer.

1 boring towns in Cornwall ☐

2 terrible days in Boscastle ☐

3 people who live in Boscastle ☐

b) Find the words in the text and underline them. Circle the right German word.

1 harbour: *Parkplatz, Hafen, Teich*

2 disaster: *Königin, Feinde, Katastrophe*

3 flood: *Überschwemmung, Brand, Schnee*

4 damaged: *erneuerte, erbaute, beschädigte*

c) Answer in English.

1 Where's Boscastle? ______________________

2 Write five things you can see in Boscastle. ______________________

____

3 What was the disaster in 2004? ______________________

4 How many people died? ______________________

▸ S. 88

20 WRITING

You're on holiday.
Write an e-mail to your American penfriend.
The questions in the box can help you.

- Where are you?
- What's in the town/village?
- What do you think of it?
- What's it famous for?
- What have you bought?
- What did you do yesterday?
- What are you doing tomorrow?

▸ S. 89

CHECKPOINT

Past perfect

Trage hier den Checkpoint aus dem Schülerbuch (Seite 91) ein und schreibe deine eigenen Beispielsätze auf.

Wenn zwei Handlungen in der Vergangenheit passieren, steht die ____________________

Handlung im *past perfect*.

Das *past perfect* wird gebildet mit ______________ und dem ________________________

______________________________.

Meine Beispielsätze: ____

____

► S. 91

21 **Jasmine is talking about her holiday in Newquay last month.**
Read the sentences and look at the pictures.
What happened first and what happened second? Write 1 and 2.

1 After we had stayed in Truro for two days, we went to Newquay.

2 After we had had lunch in Newquay, we went to the beach.

3 I had tried surfing in Truro before I visited Newquay.

4 We stayed in B and Bs because my friend had given me their addresses.

5 Before we went to Cornwall, I had read lots of tourist brochures.

► S. 91

22 **Luke and his mum. Pick the right form of the verbs: simple past or past perfect?**

When Luke came home yesterday, he ________ *(was / had been)* tired because he ____________ *(played / had played)* football all afternoon. His mum ________ *(was / had been)* angry because Luke ______________ *(fell / had fallen)* and his clothes were really dirty. "And did you remember to go shopping for me?" she __________ *(asked / had asked)*. But Luke _________________ *(forgot / had forgotten)*. "That's it! You're grounded for a week!" _________ *(said / had said)* his mum.

▸ S. 91

23 **Olivia wanted to be in a surfing competition last Sunday.**
Finish her e-mail to her friend Isaac with verbs in the past perfect.

Hi Isaac,

The surfing competition was a disaster! We arrived late. Dad *hadn't driven (not drive)* to Cornwall before, and the roads were busier than he _________________ *(think)*. When the competition started, I was so embarrassed – I found I ____________ *(leave)* my surf-board at home! I ____________ *(tell)* Dad to put it in the car, but he _________________ *(not hear)* me. So I couldn't be in the competition and we ______________ *(go)* all the way to Cornwall for nothing!

Bye, Olivia

▸ S. 91

24 **Ryan is talking about last Saturday. Write his sentences.**

First ...	Then ...
1 I gave the cat some food.	I had my breakfast.
2 I drank my tea.	I went into town.
3 I tried on seven jackets.	I bought some flip-flops.
4 I left the clothes shop.	I had lunch in a cafe.
5 I ate a sandwich.	I went home.

1 *After I had given the cat some food, I had my breakfast.*

2 *After I* ______________________________

3 *After I* ______________________________

4 ______________________________

5 ______________________________

▸ S. 91

TEST YOURSELF

1 In the kitchen. Write the words.

1 ______________ 5 ______________

2 ______________ 6 ______________

3 ______________ 7 ______________

4 ______________ 8 ______________

2 Say it in English.

1 Was bedeutet das? ______________________________

2 Wo gibt es Besteck? ______________________________

3 Ich möchte die Jeans anprobieren. ______________________________

3 In the street. Write these dialogues.

1 station, / me, / where's / excuse / please / the / ?

____

2 King Street, / the / opposite / it's / park / in / .

____

3 are / from / where / you / ?

____

4 England / the / I'm / in / south / of / Cornwall, / from / .

____

4 On holiday. Finish the sentences.

had been • had had • had met • had swum • bought • was • went • wrote

Yesterday, after we ____________ breakfast, we ____________ to the beach. I ____________ tired at lunchtime because I ____________ in the sea. After we ____________ to a cafe, I ____________ some text messages. Then I ____________ an ice cream in the cafe because I ____________ a nice girl there at lunchtime – but she wasn't there. Maybe tomorrow ...

▸ Die Lösungen findest du auf Seite 72 .

TEST YOURSELF – LÖSUNGEN*

Wenn du Probleme bei der Punktevergabe hast, bitte deine Lehrerin / deinen Lehrer um Hilfe.

Unit 1

1 Put in *some* or *any*.

some, any, any, some, some, any

Gib dir für jedes richtige Wort 0,5 Punkte.
Deine Punktzahl:

2 Asking for information.

1 ... *help me, please?*
2 ... *to Big Ben?*
3 ... *I get tickets for the London Eye?*
4 ... *that, please?*
5 ... *the tickets, please?*

Gib dir für jeden richtigen Satz 1 Punkt.
Deine Punktzahl:

3 Write the verbs ...

I*'m having* lots of fun.
We*'re sitting* on the beach at the moment and my cousin *is playing* his guitar.
My parents *are buying* some ice cream.
Are you *going* on holiday this summer?

Gib dir für jede richtige Lösung 1 Punkt.
Deine Punktzahl:

4 Simple present. Circle the right words.

goes; don't; go; don't; go; do

Gib dir für jede richtige Lösung 0,5 Punkte. Deine Punktzahl:

Zähle alle Punkte zusammen. Von insgesamt 16 Punkten hast du erreicht:

TESTERGEBNIS

16–14 Punkte:
Du bist richtig fit in Englisch. Mache weiter so!

13,5–11 Punkte:
Deine Englischkenntnisse sind gut. Versuche die kleinen Fehler noch zu vermeiden.

10,5–8 Punkte:
Du kannst schon recht gut Englisch. Aber: du musst noch genauer lernen, um besser zu werden.

7,5–5 Punkte:
Du kannst einiges in Englisch. Leider hast du noch einige Lücken. Frage deine Lehrerin / deinen Lehrer, wie du diese Lücken schließen kannst.

4,5–0 Punkte:
Leider hat es dieses Mal nicht so gut geklappt. Du hast noch erhebliche Lücken. Frage deine Lehrerin / deinen Lehrer, wie du diese Lücken schließen kannst.

UNIT 2

1 *Much* or *many*?

many, much, many, much, much

Gib dir für jedes richtige Wort 0,5 Punkte.
Deine Punktzahl:

2 Put the sentences ...

4, 1, 5, 3, 2

Gib dir für jede richtige Lösung 1 Punkt.
Deine Punktzahl:

3 Read Harry's e-mail.

1 ✗ 2 ✓ 3 ✓
4 ✗ 5 ✓

Gib dir für jede richtige Lösung 1 Punkt.
Deine Punktzahl:

* Bei der Bewertung der Übungen mit Punkten wurde in der Regel nach folgenden Kriterien vorgegangen: Für ein Lösungswort, das nur zugeordnet werden muss, gibt es 0,5 Punkte. Bei einem selbstständig zu schreibenden Lösungswort oder einem Satz, der nur zugeordnet werden muss, 1 Punkt, bei der selbstständigen Formulierung eines ganzen Satzes 2 Punkte.

4 Last Saturday. Write the verbs.

did you go, went, were, didn't come, did you do, played, bought, watched, didn't win

Gib dir für jede richtige Lösung 1 Punkt.
Deine Punktzahl:

**Zähle alle Punkte zusammen.
Von insgesamt 21,5 Punkten hast du erreicht:**

TESTERGEBNIS

21,5–18,5 Punkte:
Du bist richtig fit in Englisch. Mache weiter so!

18–16 Punkte:
Deine Englischkenntnisse sind gut. Versuche die kleinen Fehler noch zu vermeiden.

15,5–11,5 Punkte:
Du kannst schon recht gut Englisch. Aber: du musst noch genauer lernen, um besser zu werden.

11–9 Punkte:
Du kannst einiges in Englisch. Leider hast du noch einige Lücken. Frage deine Lehrerin / deinen Lehrer, wie du diese Lücken schließen kannst.

8,5–0 Punkte:
Leider hat es dieses Mal nicht so gut geklappt. Du hast noch erhebliche Lücken. Frage deine Lehrerin / deinen Lehrer, wie du diese Lücken schließen kannst.

UNIT 3

1 Look at the picture.

1 a *church*
2 a *bridge*
3 a *shop*
4 a *post office*
5 a *car park*
6 a *tourist office*

Gib dir für jedes richtige Wort 1 Punkt.
Deine Punktzahl:

2 Circle the right word.

1 *these*
2 *those*

Gib dir für jedes richtige Wort 1/2 Punkt.
Deine Punktzahl:

3 Read the questions ...

1 *No, it was on special offer.*
2 *No, it's a waste of time.*
3 *Yes, I bought it last Friday.*
4 *Yes, because I bought some cider last week.*

Gib dir für jede richtige Lösung 1 Punkt.
Deine Punktzahl:

4 What do teenagers think ...

1 *have to*
2 *don't have to*
3 *can't*
4 *can*
5 *can't*
6 *have to*

Gib dir für jede richtige Lösung 1 Punkt.
Deine Punktzahl:

**Zähle alle Punkte zusammen.
Von insgesamt 17 Punkten hast du erreicht:**

TESTERGEBNIS

17–15,5 Punkte:
Du bist richtig fit in Englisch. Mache weiter so!

15–13 Punkte:
Deine Englischkenntnisse sind gut. Versuche die kleinen Fehler noch zu vermeiden.

12,5–10 Punkte:
Du kannst schon recht gut Englisch. Aber: du musst noch genauer lernen, um besser zu werden.

9,5–7,5 Punkte:
Du kannst einiges in Englisch. Leider hast du noch einige Lücken. Frage deine Lehrerin / deinen Lehrer, wie du diese Lücken schließen kannst.

7–0 Punkte:
Leider hat es dieses Mal nicht so gut geklappt. Du hast noch erhebliche Lücken. Frage deine Lehrerin / deinen Lehrer, wie du diese Lücken schließen kannst.

UNIT 4

1 Sarah is writing an e-mail ...

me, it, him, them, us

Gib dir für jedes richtige Wort 1 Punkt.
Deine Punktzahl:

2 Match the words.

2 *amusement arcade*
3 *charged up*
4 *take off*
5 *roller coaster*
6 *internet kiosk*

Gib dir für jedes richtige Wort 0,5 Punkte.
Deine Punktzahl:

3 Tim, your British friend, is staying ...

Tim sagt *ja, (gern)* – er *hat Hunger*.
Er sagt, er hätte gern ein Brot mit *Käse*.
Er fragt, *ob du Milch hast*.

Gib dir für jede richtige Lösung 1 Punkt.
Deine Punktzahl:

4 Finish the sentences.

2 *I'll close*
3 *I'll turn off, won't waste*
4 *I'll find*
5 *I'll buy*
6 *won't make*

Gib dir für jeden richtigen Satz 1 Punkt.
Deine Punktzahl:

Zähle alle Punkte zusammen. Von insgesamt 16,5 Punkten hast du erreicht:

TESTERGEBNIS

16,5–14,5 Punkte:
Du bist richtig fit in Englisch. Mache weiter so!

14–11,5 Punkte:
Deine Englischkenntnisse sind gut. Versuche die kleinen Fehler noch zu vermeiden.

11–8 Punkte:
Du kannst schon recht gut Englisch. Aber: du musst noch genauer lernen, um besser zu werden.

7,5–5 Punkte:
Du kannst einiges in Englisch. Leider hast du noch einige Lücken. Frage deine Lehrerin / deinen Lehrer, wie du diese Lücken schließen kannst.

4,5–0 Punkte:
Leider hat es dieses Mal nicht so gut geklappt. Du hast noch erhebliche Lücken. Frage deine Lehrerin / deinen Lehrer, wie du diese Lücken schließen kannst.

UNIT 5

1 Write the words.

1 *kids*
2 *ago*
3 *the high jump, running*
4 *furniture*
5 *big/busy*
6 *Wales, Northern Ireland*

Gib dir für jede richtige Lösung 1 Punkt.
Deine Punktzahl:

2 Liam's lessons on Monday.

1 *second*
2 *fourth*
3 *first*
4 *third*

Gib dir für jedes richtige Wort 1 Punkt.
Deine Punktzahl:

3 Find the partners.

2 *You're welcome.*
3 *really bad*
4 *That's wrong.*
5 *It isn't hard.*
6 *great*

Gib dir für jede richtige Lösung 0,5 Punkte. Deine Punktzahl:

4 **Write the sentences …**

1 *If my friend moves back to Spain, I'll be devastated.*
2 *If I come third in the competition, I won't worry.*

Gib dir für jede richtige Lösung 2 Punkte.
Deine Punktzahl:

Zähle alle Punkte zusammen. Von insgesamt 18,5 Punkten hast du erreicht:

TESTERGEBNIS

18,5–16 Punkte:
Du bist richtig fit in Englisch. Mache weiter so!

15,5–12,5 Punkte:
Deine Englischkenntnisse sind gut. Versuche die kleinen Fehler noch zu vermeiden.

12–9 Punkte:
Du kannst schon recht gut Englisch. Aber: du musst noch genauer lernen, um besser zu werden.

8,5–6 Punkte:
Du kannst einiges in Englisch. Leider hast du noch einige Lücken. Frage deine Lehrerin / deinen Lehrer, wie du diese Lücken schließen kannst.

5,5–0 Punkte:
Leider hat es dieses Mal nicht so gut geklappt. Du hast noch erhebliche Lücken. Frage deine Lehrerin / deinen Lehrer, wie du diese Lücken schließen kannst.

UNIT 6

1 **In the kitchen.**

1 *potatoes*
2 *carrots*
3 *onions*
4 *butter*
5 *plate*
6 *knife*
7 *fork*
8 *spoon*

Gib dir für jedes richtige Wort 1 Punkt.
Deine Punktzahl:

2 **Say it in English.**

1 *What does that mean?*
2 *Where's the cutlery?*
3 *I would like to try on the jeans.*

Gib dir für jede richtige Lösung 2 Punkte.
Deine Punktzahl:

3 **What goes together?**

1 *Excuse me, where's the station, please?*
2 *It's in King Street, opposite the park.*
3 *Where are you from?*
4 *I'm from Cornwall, in the south of England.*

Gib dir für jeden richtigen Satz 1 Punkt.
Deine Punktzahl:

4 **On holiday.**

had had; went; was; had swum; had been; wrote; bought; had met

Gib dir für jede richtige Lösung 1 Punkt.
Deine Punktzahl:

Zähle alle Punkte zusammen. Von insgesamt 26 Punkten hast du erreicht:

TESTERGEBNIS

26–22,5 Punkte:
Du bist richtig fit in Englisch. Mache weiter so!

22–17 Punkte:
Deine Englischkenntnisse sind gut. Versuche die kleinen Fehler noch zu vermeiden.

16,5–11,5 Punkte:
Du kannst schon recht gut Englisch. Aber: du musst noch genauer lernen, um besser zu werden.

11–7,5 Punkte:
Du kannst einiges in Englisch. Leider hast du noch einige Lücken. Frage deine Lehrerin / deinen Lehrer, wie du diese Lücken schließen kannst.

7–0 Punkte:
Leider hat es dieses Mal nicht so gut geklappt. Du hast noch erhebliche Lücken. Frage deine Lehrerin / deinen Lehrer, wie du diese Lücken schließen kannst.